The Blinks
'Sad'

By Andrea Chatten

Illustrations by Rachel Pesterfield

Copyright © 2017 Andrea Chatten

The rights of Andrea Chatten to be identified as the author of this work have been asserted in accordance with the Copyright, Designs and Patents Act. All rights reserved.

First published in 2017 by
Solopreneur Publishing

www.thesolopreneur.co.uk

The publisher makes no representation, expressed or implied, with regards to the accuracy of the information contained in this book, and cannot accept any responsibility or liability.

Except for the quotation of small passages for the purposes of criticism and review, no part of this publication may be reproduced, stored in a retrieval system, or transmitted, in any form or by any means, electronic, mechanical, photocopying, recording or otherwise, except under the terms of the Copyright, Designs and Patents Act 1988 without the prior consent of the publisher at the address above.

ISBN 978-0-9931880-7-7

Printed in the U.K.

For further copies please go to - www.oodlebooks.com.

Also available on Amazon and Kindle.

Dedication

This book is dedicated to my best friend and husband Simon, for all your love, support and wonderfulness.

CONTENTS

Chapter 1 – Shan

Chapter 2 – Erasers

Chapter 3 – Opposites

Chapter 4 – Parents' evening

Chapter 5 – Blinktastic

Chapter 6 – Evidence

Chapter 7 – Calm

Chapter 8 – Time for honesty

Chapter 9 – Tweak a boo

Chapter 10 – Hidden messages

Chapter 11 – The meeting

Chapter 12 – Brain circuits

Chapter 13 – Doing things differently

Chapter 14 – Back to old ways

Chapter 15 – New friends, new lifestyles

Chapter 16 – The future

Chapter 1
Shan

Meet Shan.

Why did that have to happen? I am a failure! I can't stop thinking about that sad time... or that sad time. Or that sad time... Nothing ever goes right for me. I have no interest in doing anything. My life is boring! Why do bad things always happen to me?

Shan is 11 years old and is the oldest pupil at Croft House School due to her birthday being on 1st September. Although many of her year group wished they were one of the oldest, Shan never liked it. She was once told that if she had been born the day before, 31st August, then she would have had to go to school for one whole year less! This thought, along with so many others, stuck in Shan's brain and as you can imagine, made her feel sad most of the time.

Little did she realise that John in Y4 did have his birthday on 31st August! He also didn't like it, as he *was* the youngest in the year! And the smallest! However, the difference between John and Shan was that John knew there was nothing he could do about it. So, when he was in Year 3, he learned to accept it and let the sad feeling go.

Sadly, Shan never realised John's side of this event. She wasn't very good at seeing that the grass isn't always greener on the other side or that she could free herself from this sad feeling. So instead, she carried this around with her like a huge grey cloud inside her heart.

This issue is just one of many that made Shan feel sad most of the time. Would you like to know some more? Here are Shan's top 10 sad facts:

1. She feels lots of bad things have happened in her life.
2. She has lots of sad memories.
3. She has no friends.
4. She is lonely.
5. She is always bored.
6. Few good things have ever happened in her life.
7. She has no hobbies.
8. Things always go wrong for her.
9. She hates her life.

10. She spends too much time thinking about sad memories.

I am sure you will agree that this list is a sad read in itself. (Don't worry if this has made *you* sad, you are reading the right book and will learn lots of ways to change your sadness as you read on!)

Imagine for a minute what it is like inside Shan's head! If we were to have a sneaky peak, what you would first notice is just how cluttered it is with sad thoughts. Our thoughts are supposed to come and go, as they are simply us guessing what is happening in the world around us. Shan never lets any of her thoughts go, so her brain and mind are totally blocked with brain junk.

There are also negative weeds tangled up everywhere in Shan's brain, which make it work slower and even stop some parts working properly. It is also very dark and dingy and between you and me, it could do with a good sort out and an even bigger clear out!

Shan spent many hours with her sadness. She often wondered what may have caused it. Sometimes she thought it might have something to do with home.

Her mum was sad a lot of the time and shared many tales of moving from China with her parents when she was a child. Mrs Wan, even after living here for over 30 years, still craved the sights, sounds and smells of her early childhood life. Shan loved hearing the tales of her heritage but the stories had an underlying unhappiness which contributed further to Shan's sadness pot.

Shan was also an only child and the issues that many of you with siblings would love to experience, Shan took for granted. For example, Shan never complained when someone was annoying her all the time! Never once did Shan feel it was unreasonable to go to bed at the time she did, which was probably earlier than older siblings if she happened to have them! And it wasn't an issue for

Shan to have a whole fish to herself when they had a takeaway for tea, rather than having to share it!

For any of you with brothers and sisters, I am sure that these issues sound familiar, and can at times be very frustrating. However, for Shan it was not having these things that made her sadder.

I am sure many of you reading this are only children too and I doubt that these issues have ever led to the deep sadness that Shan feels. This is probably because you have good friends.

We can't do anything about the family we are born into but friends, if picked right and treated well, can become the family we choose. Sadly, Shan wasn't too good at this. She wasn't always good at choosing and she certainly wasn't good at keeping!

Since starting school, Shan had moved from one difficult friendship to another. Her very first friend was when she was in nursery. Livvy was also there and together they used to play dressing up in the home corner. Shan always wanted to be the doctor and Livvy was more than happy to be the nurse for the first 200 times but on the 201st time, she decided that she would like to be the doctor!

Shan was horrified. This wasn't the game *they* played together. She was the doctor and Livvy was the nurse. Together they were a good team as Teddy had survived his many illnesses due to him getting the right medicines and being bandaged up so perfectly. Shan refused to be the nurse and even though Livvy tried very hard to put her case forward, Shan threw down the stethoscope in a moment of impatience. It splintered into several pieces.

Livvy started to cry. The other children who saw what happened ran to comfort her and Shan watched, feeling sad that no-one was being her friend at that time. The friendship between Shan and Livvy was also broken and this couldn't be fixed with sellotape.

The next friend she picked was Danielle, who was quite demanding. Shan liked that at first because she realised she had been like that with Livvy and so wanted to do things differently this time. Shan really struggled with this friendship as she felt she had no choices within it. Danielle decided everything and wanted Shan just for herself. She would even get cross if Shan went to someone else's party at the weekend.

One day in the playground, Danielle had been unkind to Shan because she couldn't go to her house after school. Truth be known, Shan hadn't even asked her mum as she just didn't want to go. Danielle was going on and on about it until suddenly, Shan reached breaking point. She shouted at Danielle to shut up and then pushed her to go away.

Mrs Bell, the dinner lady, witnessed what had just happened and marched

Shan inside. As Shan looked behind her, Danielle was surrounded by lots of children, leaving her feeling sad that no-one was there for her again.

Sadly, Shan never learned the lesson that sharing or being honest is a huge part of being a good friend and so made the same mistake many more times.

Shan didn't offer her snack to Allan when they used to play *tig* together in Year 1, even though he always offered his and Shan took it. She never told those people she liked and who had been kind to her that she valued them. Not once did she share her felt tips with the people on her table, even when the class ones had all ran out or the tips had expanded and were more like scratchy brushes! Her class mates thought she was selfish, that she didn't care about them and that she was mean.

Yet worse than all of these, Shan never shared herself. She didn't share her happiness, her fun side or her sense of humour. So, as time went on, children decided that they didn't like her and so she didn't like them. This made Shan even less generous with herself, which led to her feeling very lonely most of the time and this was likely to be another huge contribution to her sadness.

To add to this, Shan wasn't honest about who she was or how she felt. Shan felt like she wore a mask. Her mask hid the sadness she felt. It shielded others from what she was really feeling. She hid behind the fake person she had become, but sometimes the mask slipped. The children in her year group were only too aware of this falseness and it made them feel uneasy in her company as they never knew what side of Shan they might see next.

Shan wasn't being true to what she was feeling and so this also added to her sadness. As no-one knew that Shan was as sad as she was, no-one helped her or supported her during those difficult times.

This made her feel cross too, as she felt nobody cared about her and she kept these bitter feelings alive every day which made the misery grow even worse.

Many nights Shan lay in her bed drowning in tears of sadness. Countless times the sadness would pull her out of her sleep and remind her of the difficulties she faced each day. Even worse, her sadness would pair up with her imagination and become the director of horrible dreams which jolted her into the dark reality of the lonely night.

Some mornings Shan felt like she couldn't bear to feel sad anymore and some days she was scared if it wasn't there as much as usual. She really wasn't sure how to be without sadness. All in all, Shan was in a grey place with little sunshine but, at times in life, things need to get worse before they get better.

Chapter 2
Erasers

Shan woke up that Tuesday morning with the same heavy sadness that she felt most days. "Who am I going to be today?" she asked herself. Will I be lonely? Will I be angry? Will I be dull? Shan knew the reality was that she would be all of these things at some point during the day.

She dragged herself out of her warm bed. She used to see her bed as a safe place but recently it had become the film set for unpleasant dreams and intense feelings. Her mum had noticed the increase in night terrors but put them down to her age, not understanding the reality of what Shan was really feeling.

Shan looked at herself in the mirror. Her eyes looked dead. They were also staying half closed as if she didn't want people to see her reality. Her mouth was beginning to hang down permanently. Her eyebrows wrinkled in the middle. This was what sat behind the mask.

Shan brushed her teeth half-heartedly and picked up the clothes that lay in a pile on the floor from yesterday. She knew there was tomato sauce on the sleeve of her jumper but couldn't be bothered to get a clean one out. She headed downstairs, smoothing her hands over her jet-black bobbed hair.

"Morning Shan. Cereal or toast?" asked Mum.

"I'm not hungry." replied Shan.

"You haven't had breakfast for a couple of weeks now, Shan. You need breakfast. It is the fuel to get you through until lunch."

"I just can't eat on a morning anymore. I feel too sick."

"It doesn't help that you eat so much at supper time Shan. I think we need to stop supper and go back to breakfast like other children your age. This really isn't good for you and I am sure it is why you are having more night terrors. You had one last night again. I heard you thrashing around and shouting. Your body can't have good sleep if it is trying to digest a full tummy. So tonight, no supper. Do you hear me, no supper?" warned Mum.

Shan could only hear noise. Her mum did this a lot. It went on and on and on until Shan just switched off and all she could hear was blah, blah, blah!!!!

"Shan, did you hear me?"

"Yes, yes I heard you. Okay, whatever."

"Don't take that tone of voice with your mother, Shan. She does a lot for you. Show her some respect," said Dad as he wandered into the kitchen grabbing his car keys ready to leave for work.

Shan sighed. Now Dad was having a go at her too. Was this what being a kid was all about? People on your back all the time and nobody really getting it from your side? This was when she really missed having a brother or sister, someone she could roll her eyes at or have a whinge to about Mum and Dad.

"We have parents' evening tonight Shan, so we'll meet you at school as we have one of the earlier appointments. Please don't forget. It is important that you are there," explained Dad firmly.

Shan's heart thumped in her body.

Shan dreaded parents' evening.

Last year, Mrs Ramsey told her mum and dad that she was worried about Shan as she had no friends and seemed to have lost interest in school work. When they all got home, Shan was told very seriously that school work was her main priority and that in future, all homework had to be shown before it went back to school to make sure that it was of a high enough standard.

The friends' thing wasn't seen to be important to them. School was a place to work hard and learn, not play. It was a big thing to Shan though, and probably the biggest thing of all which affected her sadness. This year however, Shan had another issue that she was fearful Mum and Dad might find out about.

Last week, Shan had been found with two brand new school rubbers in her school bag. Here's how it all came about.

*****

It was a usual sad day for Shan. Nothing was going right and no-one was her friend. At lunchtime she had asked her teacher if she could stay in and tidy the classroom.

Mr Pryce knew how lonely Shan was and often worried that she seemed very sad for a child her age but wasn't sure why or how to help. He had mentioned it to the Psychologist (the person in school who helps teachers to understand children's problems better) only the day before, who agreed to have a chat with Shan to see if there were any problems. Due to all of the sadness, he said yes.

"When you have given the classroom a quick tidy Shan, would you mind starting on the stock cupboard? We had lots of new stock delivered last week and I haven't had chance to tidy it so that I can put it all away. It just needs everything straightening up and any scruffy paper or empty boxes putting into the recycling bin. Are you okay with that?" asked Mr Pryce.

"Yes Sir, of course." Shan really like Mr Pryce. He was funny, kind and always had some great stories from when he was younger. He was also quite strict too and although he didn't shout very often, when he did you really did stop and listen.

Shan was eager to do this job for her teacher and was delighted to have been given something which might just distract her from her sadness for a while. She started immediately.

First the classroom. All the table pots were put neatly into the centre of each table and any rubbish from the floor put into the correct bin. She straightened the books on the book shelf and then stood the World War 2 topic books up as they were supposed to be, like soldiers guarding the artefacts that the children had donated to the special table.

When she looked around the classroom,

she felt satisfied that it was tidy enough. So, now for the stock cupboard.

Mr Pryce was right, it definitely needed a sort out. There were half-empty pencil boxes on top of reams of A4 paper. There were exercise books of different colours dumped on spare shelf space. This was going to be a pleasure.

Shan rolled up her sleeves and started with vigour. First she put all the new unused pencils together. That got rid of four cardboard boxes straight away. Then she did the same with coloured pencils, felt tips, rulers and rubbers. It was the white school rubbers that stopped her flow.

If they had been rubbish rubbers, she would have just carried on but these were those very white, soft erasers which you know will rub out really well. Shan held one in her hand. She then took a pencil and drew a squiggle on a piece of scrap paper. She was right. With very little effort the pencil scribble disappeared, just leaving grey eraser worms on the paper.

Shan had never used a brand new rubber before. She had never owned a rubber as good as that before either. Now it was used, it felt like it belonged to her. At that time, right or wrong didn't even come into her mind. The only thought she had was that no-one could love that rubber as much as she could. She deserved something nice, seeing that most of her life made her sad. This rubber had made her happy, she needed it.

This is where things went very wrong.

She held the slightly used rubber that was in her hand and then grabbed another new one from the box. Although her heart was pounding, she wasn't feeling sad at that moment. In fact, it was the first time in a long time that she felt alive. She headed out into the cloakroom and stuffed the two rubbers into the front pocket of her bag just as someone came in. She didn't have time to zip up the pocket fully and her guilt made her feel very exposed.

She quickly left her bag and headed back into the classroom to continue with the stock cupboard job. Deep inside her mind, she knew that what she had done was wrong but, at this time, it all felt very right.

Mr Pryce was delighted when he brought the children back into classroom after lunch and praised Shan in front of the whole class. "You're hired," he said pointing his finger seriously at her. "If you would like to stay in every lunchtime this week Shan, you can have that special job and when it is finished, there will be lots of house points for your team."

A cheer rang out from everyone who was in Shan's house of Sheaf. Shan felt a new feeling; one that felt very alien to her. She even felt her mouth turn upwards very slightly though this felt more weird than anything else.

She sat down in her seat and was greeted by her table like she was a celebrity. This was the feeling that she was missing. This was the feeling that she craved. This was one of the feelings that could replace sadness.

Suddenly, an urgent panic hit her and she realised what she had done earlier. Her face went pale. Her eyes flashed with fear. She then realised what she needed to do, but how could she do it without being noticed or worse still, without being caught?????

Chapter 3
Opposites

Mr Pryce took the register and everyone answered their names in French, just like they did every other day. However, this wasn't like every other day for Shan. As she sat, her brain was chattering away at hundreds of thoughts a minute. The difference today was that not all of them were sad.

Scared and nervous were just some of the thoughts flooding her mind at that moment, due to what might happen if she was found out before she could put things right. Some thoughts were angry, yes some were very angry: angry at herself for doing something so stupid, especially today. Some feelings were more positive, but these had now been shoved to the bottom of the pile.

Shan felt pleased at being cheered by her classmates, proud that Mr Pryce had praised her so much and happy that for the first time in a long time, she felt something other than sad. Yet due to this emotional cocktail, she felt sick, really sick.

Marcus had sat opposite Shan every day since September and could see that something wasn't right with her. She usually looked weak, her shoulders dipped, her head hung low. Marcus once thought that Shan looked like a drawing as she was so slow and flat, almost not lifelike.

Today Marcus picked up an energy from Shan that concerned him. He could almost hear cogs turning in her brain but, more than that, she looked agitated, animated but also pale with a slight tinge of green!

"Are you okay, Shan?" asked Marcus, unsure of what response he might get today. Sometimes she just looked through him like he wasn't there. Other days she snapped at him instantly just for breathing.

"No Marcus, I don't feel very good. I feel really sick."

Marcus jumped up and ran over to Mr Pryce, who was at his desk pulling up this afternoon's PowerPoint presentation.

"Mr Pryce, Mr Pryce, I think Shan is going to be sick. She really doesn't look very well."

Just as he lifted his head towards the direction where Shan was sitting, he saw her head out of the door very quickly with a hand covering her mouth.

"Kelsey, could you follow Shan please and check that she is okay?"

Marcus was so relieved at this point. He really wasn't that good with sick.

"Yes Mr Pryce, of course," replied Kelsey moving swiftly towards the classroom door and out of the mobile hut.

"Right children, where were we?" started Mr Pryce, bringing the afternoon's drama to a close. "So, Ancient Egypt..."

Outside, Shan felt dreadful. She had tried to retch a few times but nothing was coming out, as it is impossible to vomit negative emotions. Her hands felt clammy and her forehead was sweaty. She slumped onto the benches outside the doorway and into the upper school toilets, her head in her hands.

What was she going to do?

Then Kelsey turned up. "Mr Pryce has sent me to see if you are feeling alright. Do you want me to do anything?"

Shan smiled a quarter smile. Kelsey and Shan had never had much to do with each other in the past. Shan thought Kelsey was too popular and nice to want anything to do with her!

"Do you want me to get Mrs Dainty, the

Opposites

first aider?"

"No, no it's fine. I think I maybe just needed some fresh air," answered Shan.

"Ahh okay. Would you be alright if I just nip to the toilet please? I drank loads of water and lunchtime and was having too much fun to go before the bell went. I didn't dare ask Mr Pryce, especially with it being straight after lunch. I might as well make the most of being here now!"

Shan nodded weakly.

As Kelsey popped in through the main building door, a lightbulb moment occurred to Shan and she realised that her being out of the classroom at this moment could help her solve the whole problem and get the rubbers back to where they needed to be. She picked herself up and headed back across the yard to her mobile classroom.

She didn't have long. She opened the door of the mobile. The sound of both classes learning could be heard in the cloakroom between. The cloakroom was a mess as usual. Most of her classmates simply throw their coats towards their peg in the hope that some magic power will catch it and then float it gently to the correct place. Shan moved towards where she last saw her bag. It wasn't there. She quickly moved some coats and checked other people's pegs. Where was it?

She moved cold, damp coats from the floor and kicked aside random PE shoes. Then she saw it. The strap was peeping out under other bags. It must have been knocked off and buried in the after lunchtime madness! She pulled at the strap and freed up her school bag.

As she pulled, bags scattered across the floor. So did some of her PE kit, a few letters that she had forgotten to hand in and the rubbers. She grabbed the other things, stuffed them back into her bag and put it back in the right place. She then grabbed the white rubbers with the school logo in full view and slipped them into her pocket.

"Have you stolen those rubbers?" asked Kelsey, who had walked back into the mobile only seconds before, but couldn't fail to see that Shan was holding school property.

Shan didn't know what to say, especially not quickly. She said nothing.

"Aggghhhhh, I am telling," said Kelsey, overcome with shock that she had caught a thief in action.

"No wait," shouted Shan. "Let me explain."

It was too late. The classroom door shut. She could hear Kelsey saying something to Mr Pryce. Then she heard him shout at the class that he needed to leave for a minute but could the class please work independently and show how grown up they now were.

Then the classroom door opened. Mr Pryce walked over very calmly towards

Shan.

"Okay Shan, you know what this is about. Kelsey seems to believe that you have stolen a couple of erasers from the classroom. I really hope that she is wrong. Have you stolen two rubbers, Shan?"

"No Sir, well yes but no," mumbled Shan.

"Well is it a yes or is it a no? I think it might be better if you empty your pockets for me please."

Shan looked terrified.

She slowly slipped her hand into the left pocket. She pulled out two sweet wrappers from the night before and some grey trouser fluff.

"And the other pocket please," asked Mr Pryce, desperate for Kelsey to be wrong.

Shan gulped. The colour drained from her face once again. She slipped her hand inside the right pocket. She could feel the angular smooth erasers touch her skin.

She pulled her hand out very slowly under the piercing glare of Mr Pryce. As she removed her hand, one eraser fell to the floor and plonked onto a pile of abandoned coats.

Shan looked at the rubber. Mr Pryce looked at Shan. Shan looked at Mr Pryce. Mr Pryce looked at the rubber.

"Anything else?" asked Mr Pryce with a

very serious tone.

Shan grasped the second rubber in her hand and took it out from her pocket. She held her hand open in front of Mr Pryce.

Mr Pryce shook his head. "I am truly saddened by this, Shan. I really trusted you earlier and this is how you have repaid me. We need to go and speak to Mr Jones (the Headteacher) straight away. Come with me please."

Mr Pryce opened the classroom door and explained that he needed to do something urgently. He also popped into Mr Mullins' classroom next door to say he needed to leave his class for a few minutes and to ask him to please keep an eye on the children for him.

Mr Pryce and Shan walked over to the main building in the direction of Mr Jones' office. Neither of them spoke. Mr Pryce was gutted. He had so wanted to help Shan, which is why gave her the special job. Normally in situations like this he would get cross, but this was different and he felt genuinely saddened.

Shan felt the saddest she had ever felt. It made her realise how many times in the past she had been sad just for being sad without anything to feel really sad about. She was also really scared. Why hadn't Mr Pryce shouted at her? Why wasn't he really cross?

As they reached reception, Shan felt tears rolling down her cheeks. Mr Pryce heard a sniff.

"Why did you do it, Shan?"

"I don't know. I just did it. They were so new and so lovely. I just wanted them. I know stealing is wrong but for that moment my brain stopped working and I just did it."

"You could have put them back when your brain started working again. Or hasn't that happened yet?"

"It did. I was. When I ran out feeling sick

Sir, that was real. I suddenly realised what I had done, especially as I had just felt the best feeling ever: pride. All these different emotions made me feel ill. When Kelsey caught me in the cloakroom, I was getting the rubbers to put in our table pot. I was Mr Pryce, honestly."

Shan started sobbing. Something about what she had said and how she had said it convinced Mr Pryce she was telling the truth.

"Right. I need to do some serious thinking about this, Shan. Let's not talk to Mr Jones now. I need to think long and hard about this and so do you. I am not happy about this Shan, not at all. There will be no special jobs at the moment and I will be watching you very closely for the next few days until I decide where we go from here."

Shan dropped her head in shame. This was far worse than being shouted at. Mr Pryce almost seemed disappointed in her and that was hard to take.

Opposites

   Inside the classroom, Fozia was on watch and told the class that Shan and Mr Pryce were on their way back. As they both entered, you could hear a pin drop. All eyes were on Shan. Kelsey was biting her lip and shaking her head in disgust. How could Shan recover from this? Being shouted at would be so, so easy. This punishment, though, was going to last a very long time.

*****

Chapter 4
Parents' evening

Every day that she went home after the eraser incident, Shan had expected her parents to be in a foul mood having received 'the' phone call from school. Her walk home would be filled with dread and fear. Mr Pryce's punishment really was the worst she had ever had. This feeling of disappointment and fear hanging over her was worse than being grounded for a month!

Shan sometimes wondered if she should just tell her parents everything and then she would be free from the deep, dark secret that was locked in her soul. Sometimes she imagined saying the words out loud, but them coming out as green, rotten fumes escaping from her body.

The Blinks 'Sad'

I am scared / I am in serious trouble! / I am worried / I have made a terrible mistake / I feel alone / I did something I regret / I stole something / I want to hide / Scared!

She then thought that maybe, when the poisonous smog had ended, blue sky with little fluffy clouds would surround her and her mind would become clean.

Several times she did try to tell her mum, but talking about things wasn't something Shan or any of her family really did. Shan's mum always told her that she could talk to her about anything but, on the couple of occasions that Shan tried, her mum seemed to end up telling her off when really she wanted someone to just listen and understand.

Shan had never had anyone who listened and understood. So Shan kept everything in and like all her family, she tried to look like she was coping with it all okay.

Mrs Wan shouted through from the hallway to check if Shan wanted a lift to school. Shan hated having a lift from her mum as it meant she stood in the playground on her own for 15 minutes longer. Now that she was in Year 6, she had managed to persuade her parents that she could lock the door behind her and walk to school later. So far, this had all worked out just fine.

As she continued to pack her bag, the thought of parents' evening became too much for Shan. She really couldn't do it and neither must her parents. A huge wave of anxiety overcame her and as she bent down to put her shoes on, she threw up there and then on the floor. This really shocked Shan and she slumped herself down onto the kitchen chair.

Shan looked at the vomit. She sensed the empty house. She was obviously ill; she had evidence right there in front of her all over the kitchen floor. Never had she been so pleased to be have been sick, as normally this was something she really resisted. Shan picked up the phone to ring her mum.

"Mum, I have been sick."

"Oh no! I have got a crazy busy day today with meetings - I will have to ring your dad. Leave it with me and I will get in touch with your dad. Get your pyjamas on and get back into bed until he arrives. I will ring you later. Love you."

"Love you too," replied Shan with a slight sense of relief on her face.

Ten minutes later, Dad rang. "Hello Shan. How are you feeling? I am just going to get everything sorted for today then I will be back with you. Have you been sick again?"

"No, Dad. I am just going to go to bed now. I will clean the sick up before I go."

"You go to bed. I will sort that when I come in. Get nice and cosy and try and sleep yourself better."

"Thanks Dad, see you in a while," said Shan, pleased with the fact that the real vomit proved that she was ill. As she went upstairs, she started to feel free. Maybe some of the nasty green smoke had escaped with the vomit. No way could anyone go to parents' evening now. Mum wasn't able to go as she needed to work late tonight so Dad would need to stay and look after her.

Shan put her pyjamas back on and got back into her cooled bed. She replayed the events of that morning. So much seemed to have happened already and it was only 8.48am! Within an hour, Dad returned home from work.

The first thing Shan heard from him after the clanking of the keys hitting the kitchen windowsill was "oh dear" as he was faced with the sick!

"You okay, Shan? I am just going to clean this up. Stay in bed - that is the best place for you today."

Dad was right. Bed was where she needed to be today. Bed was maybe where she needed to be more often. So bed was where Shan began to go whenever things got difficult. Over the next few weeks, Shan's attendance in school became very low.

Some days, Shan's parents insisted that she went into school to break the illness cycle. She managed maybe one day then, as soon as another appointment was made for her parents to come in, Shan felt ill again. This went on for several weeks.

Shan's parents were becoming more and more concerned about her but they both knew she wasn't faking it - they had plenty of sick as proof! They even took her to the family doctor, only for him to confirm that

Parents' Evening

lots of sickness bugs were going round and she would soon get better. She just had to drink lots of water and rest.

This situation was also bringing lots of stress to Mr and Mrs Wan. They too were struggling between them to look after Shan. Mrs Wan had been told very firmly by her work that any more sick days due to Shan being ill, now needed to be taken as holiday. This made Shan feel more sad and things were only going to get worse.

One evening, Mrs Wan asked Shan if there was anything wrong at school.

"No Mum, everything is fine."

"You would tell me, wouldn't you?"

"Yes." Shan hung her head, feeling guilty that she hadn't and couldn't share this with her mum. "I am lonely at school though, I don't have any friends."

"Right, well, as soon as you get better you can invite a friend round for tea and to play. That is something we can sort quite quickly."

If only it was that simple, thought Shan. She smiled anyway, touched by her mum's suggestion.

In school, Mr Pryce was also concerned about Shan's sudden illnesses but every time he queried it in the office, her parents had confirmed that she was ill. He sometimes wondered if it all stemmed from the stealing incident which he had done a lot of thinking about since. However, he talked himself out of that because he hadn't got cross with Shan, so thought she was okay and anyway, lots of children had been off recently with tummy upsets.

The more days Shan did not attend school, the harder it became for her to find the strength to face it. She got sadder and sadder and every day, it removed a huge chunk from her resilience pot (the pot that helps us cope with life's ups and downs). Shan started to think she was going to be like this forever but had no idea what to do to make it better.

Parents' Evening

Luckily, up in the corners of life where people rarely look, someone very little was seeing how this poor, sad child was struggling with all these difficulties and how she was stuck in the middle of something she didn't know how to change. All this misunderstanding between adults and Shan was also creating an even bigger problem. Yet this little being knew that action was needed and having observed enough of her life, they knew Shan was the right child to help.

Chapter 5
Blinktastic

Blink 26302 Marlowe Mindful

It was quickly approaching midnight in Sheffoold. If you have read any of these books before, you will know that this is a very important time, not just in Sheffoold but in every city across the world. Midnight, you see, is a time when lots of very special things happen for some very special children.

Blink 26302 Marlowe Mindful was full of excitement about observing Shan for the last few weeks. Today's events, however, had been the icing on the cake and she felt ready to activate some Blink magic. She set off to the midnight meeting.

As she approached, Marlowe Mindful

could see the gentle glow from the bakery.

You and I would never notice the soft, warm light as our eyes aren't strong enough, but the Blinks see everything much more clearly than we do, which is why they are so good at their job. As Marlowe Mindful entered, the familiar chatter hit her ears. She found her spot and the humming was starting to fade.

"Good evening, Blinks," welcomed Chief Blink. "Please can we put our hands together to celebrate all the hard work we have done over the last 24 hours. Hurray for your wonderfulness and determination to help!"

A round of applause and excited cheers rang out in the bakery. Marlowe Mindful loved the midnight meeting and never took for granted how lucky she was to be part of something so special.

"Let's not waste any more time on us this evening, let's get to where we need to be and do what we need to do," said Chief Blink. The bakery fizzed with energy.

Marlowe Mindful tiptoed to what seemed to be her regular place, the chocolate éclair trays, though she hoped after tonight that she may be able to move on. She looked at the other Blinks heading in her direction. She loved how each of them had very different styles, flecks of colour and experiences. What she loved most was that each had very similar smiles, kind ways and good hearts. She did feel like she was part of a very special club!

Tonight, however, was when Marlowe

Mindful wanted to be promoted from Stage 1 to Stage 2. Now, I think it is important for you to understand how the five stages of Blinkery happen.

Stage 1...***On the lookout!*** This stage is when the Blinks are searching for children who may need a helping hand in life. The Blinks are either busy in research, trying to find a deserving child to work with, or feel they have already found someone special.

The chocolate éclair trays in the main display cabinet are where all Stage 1 Blinkery occurs. This is where new cases are decided and the hard work begins.

If a Blink is child free, then unattached Blinks work together to create the sugar dough buffet. This involves searching for and creating left over sugary delights into a magical feast.

This is enjoyed by all the Blinks at the end of the meeting and is a lovely way of giving them the energy they need for their next day of hard work!

Stage 2...***A good start.*** At this point, the Blinks are working with a child and everything is going as hoped. These Blinks share each other's wisdom and use it to help them give the best support to whoever they are working with.

Stage 2 happens on the vanilla slice board, also in the main display cabinet and the corner furthest from the entrance to the bakery. This is most often the least busy stage of Blinkery, as very few problems are simple to solve. However, it is also one of the most positive areas, as it is all about celebrating the good.

Stage 3...***Help!*** This is the busiest area, as all projects present challenges that need to be discussed. All this important learning and guiding happens on the large wooden bread shelves that cover the entire back wall of the bakery.

The Wise Ones are very much needed here, to share past stories of the Blinks' history so that lessons can continue to be learned. It is here that the tales of legendary Blinks are kept alive, even if they are too old to still practise.

Stage 4...***Eye spy.*** When a project is complete and the child has succeeded in moving things forward to a happier place, the Blinks dwell on the fairy cake trays that sit in the window, under large white sheets of kitchen paper.

All Blinks would agree that this is one of their favourite stages. At this time, the Blinks start to feel content and proud of what they have achieved but not until they are 100% happy that all is good, do they allow themselves to start looking for the next child. Real feelings of satisfaction only begin after the checking phase has happened. The Blinks see this as a time to be readily available just in case things go wrong, as can happen when change is still new. The Blinks have two important rules at this stage:

Blinktastic

1. Each child must tell at least one trustworthy person about the difficulties they have been feeling and what they have been doing now to make things change for the better. The Blinks believe that this is crucial so that all children know they have someone they can talk to. (Also, by sharing our problems, we connect with others so that they can support us when we need it most.)

   This rule also means that the Blinks feel happy that the child is no longer alone with their problem and so they can move more happily on to the next stage. When each Blink feels sure that each child is backed by someone else, the circle of Blink magic is complete.

2. This rule is probably the most important. Children must never mention the Blinks' help. Those

who have done in the past have very quickly regretted it, as the Blinks' input stopped from that very moment when Blink magic was spoken about out loud. The Blinks' magic can, if looked after, sparkle forever in children's hearts if it remains pure and unspoilt.

Stage 5...*Whey hey!* When the Blinks have a sense of pleasure and certainty that the child has changed their circumstances for the better, a period of celebration can begin. For seven whole days after the project has ended, beginning at midnight the following day, much fun and good times begin.

At this time, the Blinks recharge all the good in their souls. This is needed to continue with the Blinks' success, especially after handing over their hearts and brains to whoever they have just been working with. The Blinks do whatever they feel will make this stage as fabulous as it can be. Some Blinks meet up with other Blinks, some stop to relax and reflect on the satisfaction of a job well done. Whatever they do, they do it because it makes them feel happy and complete, ready for their next exciting journey.

Each Blink knows this system of Blinkery instinctively and so Marlowe Mindful did as she knew so well - she headed to all her chocolate éclair Stage 1 friends. As she approached, she could hear other Blinks talking about children that they were interested in working with.

As she got closer, she realised that Blink 14147 Lulu Let-It-Go was observing a similar child to Shan. This was so unusual. Her child was also 11 and was very sad for her age. Marlowe Mindful listened in.

The young girl was very lonely and had few friends. She had also earlier last week been caught stealing a couple of rubbers in school and was now feeling much more than sad. This wasn't a similar child it was the same child. They had both been watching Shan over the last few weeks without realising it!

Oh no, thought Marlowe Mindful, as this had never happened to her before. How could she convince the Blink panel that she wanted to work with Shan very very much? This needed some serious thinking and quick!

Chapter 6
Evidence

Marlowe Mindful took her place on the éclair tray. Next to her were Will Worry-Less and Miranda Make-It-Work. She gave them both a smile.

"Are you okay, Marlowe Mindful? That isn't your usual smile," remarked Miranda Make-It-Work.

"I think so. Well actually no, I am not really. I came here this evening hopeful that I would get moved on to the next stage as I have found a perfect girl who I would love to work with."

"So why do you not look really happy? That is a really exciting thing!" chipped in Will Worry-Less.

"Well, when I was heading over here a

minute ago, I am sure that I heard Lulu Let-It-Go describe exactly the same girl as me."

"Oh!" chorused Miranda Make-It-Work and Will Worry-Less.

"You need to talk to Logan Loyal, I think this once happened to him," whispered Will Worry-Less. "I saw him earlier. I think he is one of the wise ones on the bread shelf at the moment. Why don't you go over and talk to him to see if he has any good advice for you? We will cover for you here. Now quickly, go!"

Marlowe Mindful headed off towards the bread shelves. It felt strange to be in between stages at the midnight meeting and suddenly the bakery felt very big. As she approached the back of the bakery she could hear the buzz of conversation, the Blinks eagerly sharing and helping each other with their problems.

Logan Loyal was working with a small group. Marlowe Mindful waited until he

Evidence

had finished and decided to make the most of the opportunity when he was moving to the next group.

"Excuse me, Logan Loyal. Please could I have just a moment of your time and ask for your help on something?" asked Marlowe Mindful, trying to sound more confident than she felt.

"Of course, Marlowe Mindful. Would you like to join us this evening? Are you moving to this stage?"

"Not tonight, but maybe in the next few weeks."

Logan Loyal looked intrigued. Marlowe Mindful then went on to explain the situation with Shan and that both she and Lulu Let-it-Go had recognised that she needed some Blink help.

"Well, well, well," said Logan Loyal. "This hasn't happened for a long time. In fact, the last time I remember this happening was when it was me and Mohammed Motivator."

"What do I need to do? Lulu Let-it-Go sounded just as excited as me about helping the sad girl. She is perfect for our help, just perfect and I haven't had a project that felt as good as this for a while."

"You need to prove that you have observed and thought about this more. However, just watching and thinking will not convince anyone. You need to give the facts. Back up your case with evidence. The Blink who brings the most evidence is likely to win the project. Now get back there before it's too late."

"Thank you, Logan Loyal. I will," replied Marlowe Mindful, reversing as she went. Luckily she felt that she had a good case with Shan and would do her best to keep her as her next project.

As she approached the éclair trays, she heard Mason Make-It-Happen finishing his pitch. A round of Blink applause erupted and he sat down, feeling very pleased with what he had just done and said. There

Evidence

didn't need to be much more said as a 'thumbs up' from Terry Try-Your-Best said it all.

Marlowe Mindful squeezed back into her place between Miranda Make-It-Work and Will Worry-Less.

"Have I missed much?" asked Marlowe Mindful.

"No, but I think Lulu Let-It-Go is up next," mouthed Will Worry-Less.

He was right.

"Hi everyone," began Lulu Let-it-Go. I have found a great girl to work with who is very sad. She doesn't always make very good choices and this also has an effect on her friendships. Today she stole something from school and is now in big trouble."

"Oh dear! She definitely sounds like she needs some Blink help," exclaimed Terry Try-Your-Best, the wise one of the chocolate éclair tray. "Do we all agree that this girl could do with Lulu Let-It-Go being involved?"

A mass of heads nodded around the circle. Just then, Terry Try-Your-Best noticed a nodding pause just off centre. In fact, when he looked closer it wasn't a pause, it was three very definite head *shakes.*

"We do not seem to have full agreement for this situation," said Terry Try-Your-Best. That is fine. It is always important that we go into a new project with an issue fully discussed. Could one of you please explain why you don't agree?"

Marlowe Mindful stood to her feet. She scanned the circle of Blinks who were obviously surprised by this. This wasn't how a Stage 1 meeting usually went.

"First, can I just say that I don't have a problem with Lulu Let-It-Go and what you said."

A sense of relief escaped from Lulu Let-It-Go's face.

Evidence

"In fact, I agree more than you realise. You see, I too have been watching the same girl over the last few weeks and also came here hopeful that I would be able to begin with this project."

The chocolate éclair tray broke into chatter.

"Blinks, Blinks, please can I have your attention?" asked Terry Try-Your-Best. "Although this is a highly unusual case, it has been known before. We need to let Marlowe Mindful have her chance to say why she feels this case is worthy of her interest."

The room hushed. Marlowe Mindful smiled at Lulu Let-It-Go.

"Okay. So I have been watching Shan for a few weeks. She very rarely feels anything but sad. Her brain is caught in a cycle of overthinking sad memories. This sadness, just like Lulu Let-It-Go said, stops her having many friends because people think she is moody and mean sometimes. So she isn't always a nice person to be around.

The sadness also trickles into her sleep and she regularly has night terrors which leave her feeling sick in a morning and so she rarely has breakfast. Some days this poor girl doesn't even want to get out of bed."

The Blink circle all looked on caringly and Marlowe Mindful was very touched by the supportive nods she was receiving from Lulu Let-It-Go.

"On top of this, her parents put a lot of pressure on her which adds to the sadness and over time she has lost a lot of interest in her schooling, sport and life in general. Today she was also caught stealing, as Lulu Let-It-Go explained. She is now so stricken with worry that she has become sick in order to avoid school.

Actually though, it wasn't the sadness, the sleeping, the appetite, the friendships, the lack of enjoyment in life or the avoiding school that pushed me to want to get involved. It was the fact that one week she felt something different, something better. And so she did something different. Although it didn't work for her, I believe that she is ready for us to help her, as I think she will work hard with us to make her life better."

A round of applause rang out from the group. Lulu Let-It-Go stood up.

"That was a great pitch, Marlowe Mindful. I am impressed and I agree totally with what you have said. I suppose we would normally secret vote on who we think would be best out of the two of us to continue. However, if Terry Try-Your-Best agrees, I would like to step down and offer it to Marlowe Mindful. You deserve it."

An even louder cheer exploded from the group.

Marlowe Mindful ran over to Lulu-Let-It-Go and gave her a huge hug.

"Thank you so very much. I owe you a huge favour. At any point in the future, feel free to call it in."

"No need. Your pitch was better than mine and I think you felt more passionate about this project. Luckily, as my name states, I won't hold on to this longer than I need to. There really is no bad feeling. Tomorrow is another day."

Terry Try-Your-Best hugged the girls with pride. There had been a lot of learning tonight for everyone, even elders

Evidence

like him. "Well done for that, Blinks! It has made tonight's meeting very special. However, we still have other people to share their projects too. Who is next?"

Marlowe Mindful sat back on her seat. She felt good, and ready. Just behind her she heard a scuffling noise. As she turned around, Logan Loyal was scampering back to the bread shelves. He turned his head towards her and gave a supportive wink and a salute.

That was the icing on the cake. Terry Try-Your-Best was right, there had been lots of learning tonight for all of them. Marlowe Mindful couldn't help but notice that Blinks' names really did mean something very important. Now she needed to know that hers could also do what she needed it to do!

Chapter 7
Calm

The night was cool and dark as the midnight meeting ended. As the bakery emptied, the air caused the Blinks to retract deep into their fluff in order to not feel the chill for too long. Marlowe Mindful had a lot to think about and even more to do. She decided that Shan's house was where she needed to be.

As Marlowe Mindful tiptoed through the sky, she replayed lots of the things that she had learned that evening. How impressed she was with Lulu Let-It-Go and the fact that Logan Loyal was so bothered about what she told him, that he checked up on her later on. What good friends Miranda Make-It-Work and Will Worry-Less were.

The thing that Marlowe Mindful learned the most however, and she hadn't ever made the link before, was that Blinks really were what their name suggested. She decided to perch on a lamp-post and give some thought to this new found understanding.

Marlowe Mindful started repeating her surname in different ways. "Mindful. Mindful. Miiinnnndddfffuuulll!" In fact she said it so many times that it no longer felt like her name any more, it now sounded peculiar.

She thought about her qualities and values, the things that make Marlowe Mindful unique, special, her. She was very grounded in the present. Very rarely did Marlowe Mindful worry too much about what might happen in the future. Rarely did she think negative thoughts about the past. Marlowe Mindful was very good at seeing all the wonderfulness of the here and now.

This made her feel very grateful and

lucky. Without noticing what is going on in the present time, she would definitely miss all the little things that put a smile on her face. This was what being mindful was all about. Marlowe Mindful looked up.

The sky was black, deep black. A ripple of cool night air circled around her. Then she did the very thing her name brings to mind. She looked beyond the dark and cold, and focussed on the stars. Suddenly the sky seemed bright. The moon had been switched on and sent a warm glow across the skyline. Had the moon been there all along? Or was it that Marlowe Mindful had become *mindful* of it?

She then thought about Shan. Marlowe Mindful needed to help her do the same. It was time for Shan to move away from the sad memories and the fearful future and start to live in the moment. A wave of excitement rippled through Marlowe Mindful and with that, she skipped across to the Wan family home.

The house was quiet and still. Everyone

was deep in sleep. Marlowe Mindful lifted the flap of the letter box and squeezed through. The fibre brushes tickled as she squeezed through and several giggles escaped. Dusty the cat was relaxing at the bottom of the stairs and opened an eye.

Marlowe Mindful stopped. She had to be careful with animals, as Blinks can sometimes become curious playthings to family pets and end up in some very complicated situations! Dusty stretched out but decided to stay where she was. Marlowe Mindful headed up the stairs.

A gentle snoring sound came from Mr and Mrs Wan's bedroom. That was good - they were doing what she needed them to do. A very different sound came from Shan's bed.

Shan was in the middle of a night terror. Her body was thrashing around the bed with whimpering sounds escaping from her mouth.

Marlowe Mindful moved quickly. Shan

was laid on her back, which was the perfect position for what she needed to do next. Marlowe Mindful breathed in as deeply as she could. This increased her size and then she lay face down on Shan's heart.

This was going to be a rocky ride at the start, so Marlowe Mindful gripped on to Shan's pyjamas tightly. As she held on, she gently rippled her body so that Shan's heart was being slowly massaged. After about ten tiring minutes, Shan began to slow down. When Marlowe Mindful felt it was safe, she made the move to do part two of what was needed at this time.

She tiptoed towards Shan's head. She needed to get in there. Although Shan had her mouth slightly open, this was not the best option. Marlowe Mindful knew this from experience.

She once worked with a young person, Michael, who was always scared. Scared of everything – the dark, the light, being alone, being with other people, animals, fish and cheese! This made life very difficult for poor Michael. So Marlowe Mindful decided to help him to realise that the fear thoughts in his head made all these things seem even scarier.

In order to move things on for him, she needed to weaken the fear motorway that was getting too much thought traffic in his brain. Marlowe Mindful decided to go for entry through the mouth. She gently tiptoed across the tongue. She managed to dodge the uvula (the long dangly thing at the back of the throat), but as she squeezed round the back of his tonsils, Marlowe Mindful set off a tickly irritation.

It started with a light throat cough. Marlowe Mindful tried to remain as still as possible. Then it became a stronger, deeper cough. Every time Michael coughed, Marlowe Mindful ticked his tonsils even more. In a short space of time, Michael was coughing with force and waking up the entire house.

Michael's mum got up and headed into

the bathroom for water. "Oh no," thought Marlowe Mindful, "if I get washed into his stomach I am in big trouble."

This had once happened to an older, wiser Blink and it was to be avoided at all costs. The stomach acid we all have that digests all our food strips the Blinks of their colour. The older, wiser Blink in question lived out the rest of his Blink years with patchy bleached out fluff!

Marlowe needed to be out of Michael's mouth as quickly as possible. She started dancing at the back of his throat. She then started tickling his uvula.

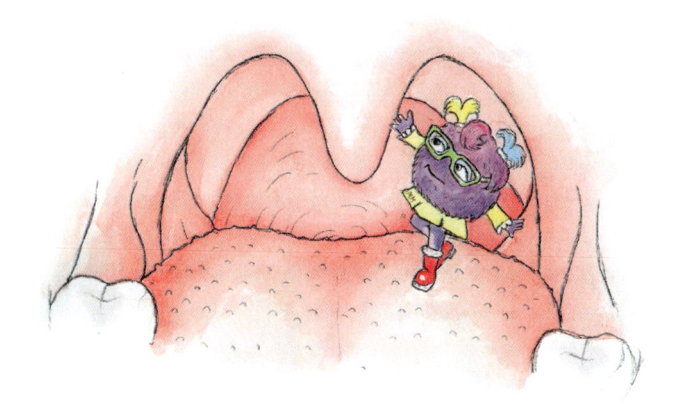

Michael began with a huge coughing spell that eventually thrust Marlowe Mindful out of his mouth right onto his mum's cheek!

"Oh well, you must feel better after that Michael," whispered Mum whilst feeling her cheek for whatever had just hit it. "It must have been some supper that had got lodged. Have some of this water and then you should be able to sleep like a log."

Michael sipped away, not quite sure what had happened or what was going on. Now though, he started feeling scared of supper and sleep.

Marlowe Mindful felt terrible. She did however manage to get done the job she intended to do that night but from that day forward, going into the mind from the mouth was to be avoided at all costs.

Marlowe Mindful brought herself back to the present. She needed to do something here and now and the night was slipping away. The quickest and easiest route was through the ear and so that was what she would do but she needed to shrink herself first.

When Marlowe Mindful was about a third of her size, she slid into the inner workings and carefully moved in towards the mind. It was very cluttered in there. Just as she had imagined, sad memories were dumped everywhere. Memories of when Shan was a toddler, her first day at school, the day she fell off her bike and scarred her knee permanently and the rubber incident from a couple of weeks ago.

Shan's happiness chemicals were also low. They were virtually empty. What Marlowe Mindful noticed most though, was that the calm part of her brain wasn't working at all. This was why she was thrashing at night - her body was making too many distressed feelings.

Marlowe Mindful moved the scattered sad memories that were covering it. She pushed them aside and blew some deep breaths on to the calm zone. This area had been deprived of oxygen for longer than she could imagine due to her negative feelings. No wonder it wasn't working properly. She kept on breathing outwards. Over time, a light pink tinge appeared. The calm zone was coming back to life.

She kept blowing. It then began to pulse. After more breaths, it began releasing calm feelings.

"Yes," yelped Marlowe Mindful. "It works again. When I introduce myself to Shan in the morning, I must teach her how to keep this important area working properly."

Marlowe Mindful looked at her tiny watch. She had a couple of hours before Shan would wake. She might as well stay there, there was plenty to do. Hopefully if she got cracking and did some tidying and tweaking, Shan might feel better as soon as she awoke.

Marlowe Mindful stayed very busy until she heard Mum's alarm go off in the distance at 7.00am. She straightened up the last pile of sad memories and headed out from where she had entered.

Shan gave a huge stretch. She wiggled and writhed underneath her duvet. Marlowe Mindful watched from behind a pencil pot on the shelf. Shan sighed. This was unusual. Normally Shan grunted the sad reality that she had to face another day with the sadness she always felt. She sat up. This was strange too. Shan usually felt like she was made of lead. Today she felt lighter.

Marlowe Mindful was pleased that the calming part of her brain was already making Shan feel better. Would what she had planned next do the same?

Chapter 8
Time for honesty

Shan lay back down on her bed. Clean air felt like it was circulating her body. A sense of calm filled her brain. She looked at the clock: 7.33am. She didn't have the same urgency on a morning anymore. School wasn't an option due to her lingering sickness. Yet for the first time in a few weeks, Shan felt like she could go.

What on earth was she thinking? This was ridiculous. The last place she needed to be was at school.

Mum popped her head round the door as she headed towards the stairs. "Morning Shan, how are you feeling today?"

"The same," replied Shan with pangs of

guilt twinging in her tummy, rather than the usual sadness and anxiety.

"Okay, sweetheart. Dad is staying around this morning and then Auntie Harriet is popping round to stay with you this afternoon. I won't be too late tonight. Love you." Mum came and planted a huge kiss on Shan's warm cheek.

"Thanks, Mum. Love you too."

Dad then shouted through from the bedroom. "I have some work to do Shan. I will be making a few phone calls for the next half hour. Do you need anything?"

"Okay, Dad. No, I am fine thanks."

This was perfect. Marlowe Mindful decided that now was the time to make herself known to Shan. This was the part that the Blinks always found the hardest. Actually starting and finishing a project had the same level of difficulty. Thinking about it now though was not going to make the doing of it any easier.

Time for honesty

As Shan lay propped up on her pillows reading her book, Marlowe Mindful tiptoed down and stood right in the middle of the opened pages.

"Hello Shan, I am Marlowe Mindful. We are going to become very good friends." Shan instinctively tried to shout for her dad but the shock of what was happening had deactivated her vocal cords.

"I was hoping that you feeling calmer this morning might make you less surprised at our introduction. Maybe some more oxygen is needed to get the calmness back again."

Shan didn't know what to do, say, think or feel. Her mind was flooding with strange thoughts as to what was going on here. Was she still dreaming? Had the imagined tummy bug finally become real and she was having some fever hallucination? Was this her sadness overwhelming her and she was actually going mad?

"No, none of the above," interrupted Marlowe Mindful. "Thoughts are just guesses, you see, and none of those guesses are right. As I said earlier, we are going to get to know each other very well. I already know you quite well, Shan. I have been with you for many weeks now, checking that you were the right child for my help."

"Really! How come I haven't seen you then?"

"Sometimes we see what we want to see.

Time for honesty

You Shan, from what I have seen so far, spend a lot of time seeing all the things in your life that make you sad, agreed?"

"How do you know all this? How did you know what I was thinking? How did you know that I was feeling calmer this morning? Do you have magic powers?"

Marlowe Mindful laughed out loud. "No, not magic. What I do Shan is very real. At times though, I must admit I do think what I can do is pretty cool. I hope you feel the same as time goes on."

Shan's eyes lit up. She was amazed at how unnerved she was with what was happening to her at this moment. She was also very aware at how rarely she was *in the moment*, so this was new for many reasons.

Marlowe Mindful continued. "Tell me about how you felt when you woke up this morning, Shan?"

"Well, when I normally wake up the first thing I think is *oh no today is going to be rubbish again.* I then very quickly start thinking of all the things that have made other days awful and before I know it I feel really sad. I always feel sad. Today I haven't got too sad yet. When I woke up this morning I felt lighter, not so heavy. I also felt stronger to face the day rather than the usual weak stressed feelings I have. I felt calmer I think."

"Good. Tell me more."

Shan couldn't believe how easily she was talking to this green-spectacled, ball of purple fluff. "As you probably know, I haven't been at school for a couple of weeks." Shan coloured up and looked away from Marlowe Mindful, feeling ashamed of what had happened in school.

"You don't need to be embarrassed about that in front of me. It is nice that you are though, it shows that you care. I know all about it. In fact it was that day that I decided that you were someone I wanted to work with. If you are strong enough to look inside yourself, Shan and

Time for honesty

brave enough to be honest, that is when you can make big changes in your life."

Shan's eyes widened. She couldn't quite believe that something good could have come out of one of the worst days of her life. She also felt relieved. She didn't have to carry this shameful darkness around with her anymore. Someone knew and they wanted to help. A tear slipped out of Shan's left eye.

"Hey you! I am not supposed to make you cry! I am here to help you feel that you can change things for the better!"

"You are. I have felt so sad and so lonely for so long that I can't remember feeling anything so good for a long time. Already I feel better. I feel like I can be honest with you and you won't hate me for it. I feel like I can be me without being judged."

Marlowe Mindful rubbed Shan's cheek. "We have a lot of work to do but I am not going anywhere until I have helped you understand your sadness better, and hopefully you will realise that it can actually be a good thing at times." As she spoke, she kicked her boot as if making a penalty shot.

"A good thing. What could be good about feeling sad?" asked Shan curiously.

"Well, sadness is telling you that something isn't right and that is always very important to know. It can also be because we love and care about people and things, and that too is valuable. The main thing to know is that without sadness, we could never feel real joy," said Marlowe Mindful. "We need sad times to help us feel truly happy and glad when we can see things are going well. If we always had the perfect happy life, it would stop feeling as good, as we would have nothing to compare it to. At times, sadness actually makes the good times awesome. You do have too much of it though Shan, so we are going to kick some of this sadness out of town!"

They both giggled. "Wow, I didn't know

Time for honesty

that. Oh, that would be great, thank you. Can I ask a question, please?" asked Shan.

"Of course," replied Marlowe Mindful. "I hope that during our time together, you ask many questions."

"You said earlier that you knew I was calmer today. How did you know that?"

"Last night whilst you were sleeping, I entered your mind. There is a lot to do in there Shan. It is very cluttered with sad memories and some parts are so deeply hidden under the brain clutter, they simply don't work. Your calm zone was one of them."

Shan looked downward again. Marlowe Mindful made her mind seem more of a mess than her bedroom and that was bad enough. "So what did you do in there?"

"Well I tidied some of the sad memories up, put them all together in the right place. I then breathed some oxygen into your calm area, as it wasn't working at all.

After a while it came back to life. It had blood flowing round it again and it started pulsing into action. This was when you started feeling calmer."

"Wowzers," said Shan excitedly. "That does sound like magic."

Marlowe Mindful gave a proud, cheeky grin. "Though I say it myself, it did all go very well!" They both giggled again.

"Do you like feeling calmer Shan?" asked Marlowe Mindful.

"I do. How can I make sure that the calm part of my brain doesn't stop working again?"

Just as Marlowe Mindful was about to begin, Dad came into the bedroom. "Do you want some breakfast, Shan? I am going down to make a cup of tea."

Marlowe Mindful quickly slid down the book and hid under a crease in the duvet. Shan covered her with interlinked fingers. "Not just yet Dad, but maybe some toast

Time for honesty

in a while please."

"Of course," said Dad kissing Shan on the forehead and nearly exposing Marlowe Mindful as his hands pressed down on the bed. "Shout if you need anything." As Dad left, both Shan and Marlowe Mindful stroked their brows, wiping away the imaginary sweat that Dad coming in had just caused.

"Phew, we were lucky there. Now couldn't be a better time to tell you how to calm the brain. I think even I need it too," laughed Marlowe Mindful. "So this is what we are going to do. You breathe in deeply for four seconds, hold the breath in for seven seconds and then breathe out slowly for eight seconds. Let's do it together."

Marlowe Mindful and Shan practised the breathing exercise several times and the more they did it, the more relaxed they felt. "This works because it stops you thinking negative thoughts, helps you focus on the present and it gets lots of oxygen to that calming part of the brain. Then you feel all fluffy and light," explained Marlowe Mindful.

"I really do feel better. Wow, if this is what I feel like after knowing you for half an hour, then I can't wait to see what else is ahead!"

"So you are on board then?" asked Marlowe Mindful.

"Absolutely," responded Shan. "Take me to happiness please."

"Fasten your seatbelt," said Marlowe Mindful. "I will see what I can do!"

Chapter 9
Tweak a boo

As the morning went on, Shan and Marlowe Mindful got to know each other better and shared many stories of each other's pasts. Shan recalled one sad memory after another and Marlowe Mindful listened and nodded as she spoke.

Although Marlowe Mindful was eager to question some of Shan's thinking, she knew that their relationship needed to be strong and the time needed to be right, otherwise Shan might feel upset that Marlowe Mindful was challenging *her* and not her thinking!

Shan was also very interested in Marlowe Mindful. She asked lots of questions and found out many amazing things about the world of the Blinks.

Shan learned how Marlowe Mindful and the rest of the Blinks of the world are created from morsels of wonderfulness that all the good people of the world leave behind when they move on from this life. This brought a tear to her eye, although she realised that it was tears of sadness and joy, as she felt that elements of her grandma and granddad, who she missed dearly, could actually be alive in the Blinks' population. This gave Shan a warm feeling of comfort.

Marlowe Mindful also revealed stories of how she got her full number title and how this was linked to each Blink's number of creation and reflected how long they had existed. Shan was fascinated to hear of Blink 347 Chez Choices, who still attended the midnight meeting at Rosie's the Bakers.

"Does she look really old? Can she still walk? How old do you think she really is?" quizzed Shan with genuine interest. "I hope I look as cool when I am over five hundred years old."

"Amazingly," continued Marlowe Mindful, "she can still do everything that a younger Blink can do. A bit slower perhaps, but the biggest difference is that she is mostly orange with tinges of purple, unlike me who is purple with flecks of orange."

"Why is that?"

"As Blinks grow in knowledge and wisdom, their fluff changes colour from purple to orange. Chez Choices is probably the wisest of Blinks at our meeting."

"So instead of getting wrinkles when you get old, you get brighter?"

"Yes, that sounds about right. I think a lot of older human beings get brighter too but sadly, it is hidden behind their aging face so you have to look harder."

"Is Blink life good?" probed Shan.

"It is the best. Doing good things for people makes us feel good. We get to meet lots of fabulous children who deserve happier times and then when we all get together at midnight, we are with people who are created from goodness and love. What could be better than that?"

Marlowe Mindful then went on to explain about all the Blinks stages of working and all the great things you get to do when a project has finished.

"I want to be a Blink," laughed Shan.

"For the moment Shan, we need to work together and you need to take all the kindness and support you can. When we have finished what we are doing, then you might get the chance to do the same for someone else."

"Yes I agree," replied Shan, feeling excited at the thought of her life feeling happier than it had done for a very long time.

"I need to head off soon Shan but, before I do, I would like you to try really hard today to not overthink sad memories. This will be really difficult to start with, but you need to be the master and not the slave! When the sad memories start creeping in try some of these things:

- distract yourself with something else, colouring, reading, thinking happier memories or even creating new thoughts of how you want to feel this time next month
- do the breathing exercise
- start saying to yourself "No. I am not thinking this today".

"Okay, but how will that help?" asked Shan.

"Sometimes when we have had sad thoughts for a long time, things start changing in the brain. You have created motorways from your sad thoughts' zone to other areas of your brain, all of which lead to deeper sadness. Together we are going to tweak what your brain does now so that it functions better. Reducing the time you spend thinking sad thoughts is step 1. So, can you give it a go and we will see how you feel next time I see you?"

"Yes of course. Thanks Marlowe Mindful. Before you go, what does 'mindful' mean?"

"Great question. Mindful is when you are in the moment with what you are doing. When you are thinking sad thoughts, Shan, you are reliving the negative past. When you are feeling anxious about life, you are putting yourself into a scary future. Being mindful is about thinking in the here and now and learning to enjoy it. Your homework is to start to become mindful."

"Yes, mindful I will become," declared Shan with a grateful smile.

"Right Shan, I need to make a move. There are some other things that I need to do in order to help you further. I will see you very soon. Work on your homework and fingers crossed we can move to step 2 next time I see you."

Shan watched as Marlowe Mindful

tiptoed out of her room and off to wherever she was needed next. Shan lay back on her bed. She couldn't believe how different she felt already. It felt like things were changing and this was before her homework!

As time went on, Shan found herself slipping into her old ways and began with the sad memories. She wasn't actually sure how long she had been thinking them before her master brain alerted her to what Marlowe Mindful had said.

"No, I am not going to think sad thoughts today or, in fact, anymore."

The sad memories were still coming. This was harder than she thought. She decided to do one of the other suggestions. She grabbed the book that she had been reading for what felt like forever. The sad memories were still there. "Be in the moment, be in the present."

Shan opened the book. She started to read. She noticed how warm her bed was.

The sad thoughts lingered. She wriggled in delight at the comfort of her favourite place. Sad memories were still there. She breathed in a deep breath, held it and let it slowly leave her as she digested the words on page 27 of her reading book. These sad thoughts weren't going anywhere.

The next time Shan was aware of what she was doing, was when she was on page 56! Where had that time gone? Wherever it had moved to, the sad memories had gone with it, because they weren't in her head at that time. How was this possible?

Shan was amazed. She had interrupted the sad process. It certainly wasn't easy but she had succeeded in the end. Marlowe Mindful was right, if she could tweak what her brain thinks then it could most definitely change what she feels.

As Shan lay there revelling in the moment, her dad popped into her bedroom and sat down on the bed.

Tweak a boo

"Have you been alright, darling? I nodded off downstairs; I don't do that very often. How are you feeling today? Ooh, it's good to seeing you doing something rather than just lying there feeling sorry for yourself."

"A little bit better I think."

"I think we need to get tough on this virus, Shan. If we leave it, it will take over. We need to be in charge of it and not the other way round. I am thinking of phoning school and suggesting we maybe try a few hours over the next few days. What do you think?"

These words didn't sound like Dad. If she didn't know any different, Shan could have sworn that Marlowe Mindful was behind this. Just as she thought this, Marlowe Mindful floated above Dad's left shoulder and gave Shan a big 'thumbs up'.

Shan looked startled.

"It's natural for you to feel nervous at the thought of it, but we will do it gently.

Whatever problems we face, we will sort them out as Team Wan!" explained Dad.

Shan sobbed and while she did, her dad just held her.

Shan wasn't sure what Marlowe Mindful had done to Dad, or what exactly it was that Dad had said to her that but, at that moment, Shan told Dad everything. Everything about school, the rubbers, Mr Pryce, her sadness and her sickness. Everything except Marlowe Mindful, of course.

Marlowe Mindful sat on the edge of the bookshelf and watched on. This was just what she wanted to happen. Dad also needed to become more mindful of the situation and of what Shan might be feeling. Dad had delivered. Now she needed to visit Mr Pryce and see if he could do the same.

Chapter 10
Hidden messages

At Croft House Primary School, things were very much the same as usual. The cloakroom was still a mess. Mr Pryce's stock cupboard was still desperate for some order. The topic table books lay like fallen soldiers. Teaching and learning was the focus, with some fun thrown in when possible.

The big difference was that no-one talked about Shan. At first, playground gossip was all about the 'rubber saga'. Then it became about Shan not coming to school because she was scared. After a while, it was mentioned now and again that Shan must be really ill to be off for this long. Sadly now though, Shan wasn't mentioned by her classmates at all.

Mr Pryce, however, still often thought about her. The niggle in his brain never left after he talked with Shan that day outside the office. He had tried to raise his concerns several times but was always faced with genuine absences confirmed by Shan's parents.

Marlowe Mindful recognised all of this and so felt confident that some intervention with Mr Pryce could be invaluable in moving this forward too. As she carefully entered the classroom, Y6P were packing up ready for lunch. She decided to squeeze on top of one of the light frames, from where she had a good view and could plan what needed to be done next.

Mr Pryce dismissed the class a table at a time and then headed over to the staff room for lunch. Brilliant, thought Marlowe Mindful. She could now start hatching a plan.

She removed her notebook from her pocket. On it was a list of possibilities.

One of them stood out more than the others. She drifted towards Mr Pryce's desk. Her mission was to place things around the room that would remind Mr Pryce of Shan.

First, Marlowe Mindful removed the two rubbers that Mr Pryce had put into his top drawer. She placed them just out of eyeshot from where he would take the register that afternoon. Obviously she didn't want the rubbers to be noticed, she wanted them to register in his deeper brain. Marlowe Mindful perched on the top of the desk chair and swung it round to a normal seated position. Yes! The rubbers could be seen but were slightly shielded by the stapler and hole punch.

Next was to find Shan's exercise books in the topic and science pile. Marlowe Mindful wanted them both to be placed at the top. Moving through the heavy, red A4 books was hard work and Marlowe Mindful nearly got squashed under the weight as she moved down the pile. Shan's book was, of course, at the bottom. This was going to be difficult but Marlowe Mindful knew what was needed.

She pushed the neat pile of books over to the right so that they collapsed into a stairway of spines. She then teased Shan's book out from the bottom like it was a Jenga block!

Shan's book eventually fell to the floor.

Marlowe Mindful picked up the book and placed it on the top of the pile. Having fluff was proving hard work; she was becoming quite hot and sweaty.

Next was to try the maths pile. This time, Marlowe Mindful went straight to the bottom and there was Shan's book as she had hoped. This was so much easier. The books were much smaller and half of them were still on Mr Pryce's desk for marking.

Marlowe Mindful decided that this one needed to be in the pile of books that Mr Pryce would be marking. She carried the book over to the desk. She was going to try and place it in the middle but had to put it down quickly when she heard the door creak open.

Mr Pryce moved towards his desk finishing the last of his sandwich. He placed his warm cup of coffee on the table and then picked up his pen ready to mark the remaining maths books.

He took the top book off the pile. Without looking, he opened it to the last work that had been done. He couldn't find today's work. He looked at the back of the book. He was amazed how many times some of the boys in his class completed work in an upside down, back to front book! No, no work there. He looked at the front for the name. It was Shan's book. A stab of sadness pricked inside Mr Pryce. He looked at the last entry in the maths book; it was nearly two weeks ago.

He marked the rest of the maths books but noticed how his mind wasn't on them as usual. Concerns about Shan had overtaken his thinking. Due to this hijacked thinking and lack of attention, Mr Pryce accidentally knocked over the last bit of his cup of coffee. The warm coffee travelled across his desk.

He grabbed whatever was going to be devoured by the brown, milky liquid. The books were moved first, then the register, followed by the cardboard box of pencils, the stapler, the hole punch and finally the erasers!

Another jab of sadness punctured his thinking - Shan. As he wiped up the coffee mess, Mr Pryce wondered why Shan was very much in his mind today. This was unusual. Marlowe Mindful looked on, was this enough or did she need to do more? *Do something* or *do nothing* came into her mind. She would keep going just to be on the safe side.

As the class returned from lunch, Mr Pryce gave instructions for them to get things ready for maths, which was the next lesson, and to recap on their times tables. He then began with the register. Marlowe Mindful was nervous of what she was going to try next but knew it was worth a try.

As the names were read from the register, a reply of "Bonjour Monsieur Pryce" was chorused by each child after their name. Marlowe Mindful was getting ready and was in a great position, peeping from behind the box of pencils. As Mr Pryce read Shan's name, a flash of purple erupted from the register.

"Whooaahh," shouted Mr Pryce.

The class looked on in surprise.

"Are you alright, Sir?" asked Zach.

Mr Pryce looked very puzzled but knew that he couldn't say this out loud. Once again, thoughts of Shan were overtaking his mind.

Marlowe Mindful sat panting behind a pile of paperwork on the other side of the desk. That took some doing. The Blinks aren't known for speed but although she said it herself, that was full on zoom!

"Yes fine thanks, Zach. Could you take the register for me please? The rest of you, off you go to maths."

Mr Pryce spent the whole afternoon in a bewildered state. Just as he was starting to feel slightly less strange Sam, one of the pupils, asked him what he should do with Shan's book as he was handing out the exercise books. Mr Pryce scrunched his face as if he was in pain.

"Put it on my desk Sam, thank you."

The afternoon seemed to go very slowly

Hidden Messages

for Mr Pryce; he felt like he was watching himself in a film. As the children left for home, he grabbed his coat and bag and headed towards the office.

He knocked on Mr Jones' door.

"Hi Mr Jones, sorry to bother you. I would like to go and visit Shan Wan on my way home this evening. She has been on my mind a lot over the last couple of weeks, but never more than today. It feels like this is something I need to do. I am worried about her."

"If you feel that strongly about this, and I can see you do, then that is what you must do. Mrs Lomas, could you ring Shan's home number please and see if it is okay for Mr Pryce to pop in on his way home?"

"Thank you. I feel I should have done something about this sooner, but today I feel I have no choice. It is almost like I have been given a sign to act today."

Mrs Lomas interrupted the conversation

flow. "No problem for you to visit. Dad is home with Shan. He was going to phone you too. The address is 94 Bercat Road."

"Brilliant. I will head there now."

"Pop and see me in the morning and let me know how it goes. You are a good teacher. Well done for acting on this," said Mr Jones, patting Mr Pryce on the back as he left.

Marlowe Mindful hitched a ride in the open front pocket of Mr Pryce's school bag. This couldn't have gone better so far. She just hoped that Shan felt the same!

Chapter 11
The meeting

In the Wan household, things had suddenly speeded up! Mr Wan was running up and down the stairs with clutter from the hallway and living room. A tidy up had been ordered by Mrs Wan when she knew of the surprise visit as she didn't want to welcome a guest into a messy home. At work she was doing her best to meet her deadline earlier than expected, as it was important to be home for most of the meeting, if not all.

Shan had managed to swing her legs out of bed and was sitting facing herself in the mirror of her wardrobe door. Why was Mr Pryce coming to see her, today of all days? She had never known of a teacher make a home visit before, so this must be serious.

Oh no, she thought a decision had been made about the stealing. She was going to be in big trouble.

Shan's thoughts bombarded her thinking for many minutes before she stopped and brought herself into the moment. Thoughts are just guesses and I have no idea what Mr Pryce is coming for but now isn't the time to let my imagination take over, she told herself. I'm not going to let my thoughts steal the first good feelings that I have had today.

Inside Shan's brain, a battle was in full swing as to who could get the most thought traffic in their area! The negative thoughts and sad memory zone was shouting for stray thoughts to come that way. Across the other side of her mind the newer and kinder, more mindful brain was offering a different way to act.

Shan felt the stronger pull towards her usual way of doing things. The familiarity and ease of doing the things that she had done so many times before was by far the

The Meeting

stronger pull. She laid down on her bed, surrendering to the sadness of the past.

She collapsed into bed. Many minutes passed before Marlowe Mindful surfaced in her memory bank. She remembered where that thinking had left her in the past. It certainly didn't make her feel good. She also remembered what Marlowe Mindful had suggested she could do when the sadness was most difficult. "No, I am not going to think like this today," she said.

She then felt a pull from the new way of thinking. She could hear Marlowe Mindful's voice inside her head reminding her how hard doing things differently would be at the start. She also heard her explaining that just because something is difficult doesn't mean you don't try, it means that you try harder!

Shan breathed in several deep breaths, held them and then exhaled very slowly. She looked herself full on in the mirror again. Today was the start of a better way of doing things. If it meant that the past had to be dealt with in order for the future to be happier, then that was what she had to do. Shan flattened her bed hair and went to the bathroom to freshen up.

On the drive to Shan's house, Mr Pryce found himself feeling quite emotional. He was nervous as to what he was going to find when he got there. He couldn't help but think how worried and sad Shan may well have been over the last few weeks. He also felt cross at himself for not acting on this sooner. Why had he not been pushier with the facts he had on Shan's attendance? Why hadn't he listened to his inner voice more?

This is something that maybe we have all done before; Mr Pryce certainly had. As he drove the distance to Shan's house, he found himself having a moment of seriousness with himself. Never would he push things aside when his head and his heart came together on something. Today was about action and he was going to make a special effort to take this newly

The Meeting

recognised lesson into tomorrow and beyond.

Marlowe Mindful was also thinking about the events of today. As she perched in the bag, unable to resist licking on the scrunched up sweet wrapper that was in there with her, she was proud of the mutterings coming from Mr Pryce as he sorted through his thoughts.

Like him, she too wondered how Shan might be since she saw her last.

Was Shan ready for moving things forward? Did she have the strength to reinstate her master brain and be in charge of what she wanted? Mr Pryce was being very mindful, she thought.

One of the most important things that we need to learn to do in life, is to name and claim what we are feeling, and Mr Pryce was doing that very well. The more we know what we are thinking, the more likely we are to know what to do with those feelings and the better the choices we will make to help them feel better too.

Mr Pryce turned onto Bercat Road. He looked hard to see what numbers the houses were where he was. 213, 211. He was too high up at the moment and Shan's house was an even number so she lived on the other side of the road. 146, 144. Not much further.

Marlowe Mindful sensed the slower pace meant they were approaching Shan's house. She wiped her lips so that no traces of daytime stickiness could be seen as it was rare for Blinks to enjoy any daytime deliciousness!

The Meeting

The car stopped and Mr Pryce grabbed his bag from the passenger seat, causing Marlowe Mindful to head-butt the soft leather of the satchel. She straightened her glasses and quickly tiptoed out of the bag as Mr Pryce swung it over his shoulder. She decided that his hood would be the best transport until they were inside. The doorbell was pressed.

Within seconds Mr Wan opened the door and gave a very calm smile, not giving any hints of what he had been doing for the last 20 minutes at all. "Please Mr Pryce, come in. Can I take your coat?"

"Thank you very much, Mr Wan. I hope Shan is feeling well enough for my visit, it would be lovely to see her too."

"Yes I will shout for her. Mrs Wan is also on her way home from work, though she said the traffic seems particularly busy. It is funny that you have chosen to come today. It is the first time that I have seen a small change in Shan. It has been a very difficult few weeks. Please come through to the sitting room. Can I get you a cup of tea or coffee?"

(Marlowe Mindful decided that Mum might need a hand to get home sooner, so headed off to see if she could help. Traffic light tweaking in times of emergencies was allowed now and then and today felt like the right day.)

"Thank you for your kindness and yes please, coffee with milk, no sugar, it has been a very busy day."

"I will go and get her. Shan, Mr Pryce is here."

Mr Pryce scanned the homely living room. He saw lots of family photographs on the windowsill. Mr Wan's newspaper was placed at the foot of his armchair. On the coffee table, it looked like the contents on top may have been straightened for his arrival.

Shan and Mr Wan entered the sitting room.

The Meeting

"Hello Shan, how are you?" asked Mr Pryce, forgetting how little and young Shan looked at times.

Shan smiled and looked at her dad, who repeated, "As I was saying earlier, it has been a difficult couple of weeks. We have been to the doctors several times but they say whatever it is will go eventually."

The kettle started gurgling from the kitchen. "Please excuse me," said Mr Wan.

Shan nervously watched her dad leave the room.

"Hey you. We have all missed you at school. I have been thinking about you a lot today too, which is why I felt I had to visit. If I am honest Shan, I wish I had called when you first went off sick. I was worried that you might be avoiding school because of what happened."

Shan looked down at her hands, feeling quite ashamed.

"Was it because of the rubbers, Shan? I

need you to be honest with me so we can sort this out and move on."

Shan nodded with a heavy head. "I have never felt so sad and scared about anything before. It did make me sick, honestly it did. Then the longer I have stayed off school, the harder it has been to come back."

"Oh, Shan. Do you want to get this sorted today? At any point when you were sorting my store cupboard, did you know that what you were doing was wrong?"

Shan started to cry. "No Mr Pryce, I promise that thought only came into my head after you had said all those lovely things about me during registration."

"What were you going to do with the erasers after you had that thought, Shan?"

"I was going to put them into our pencil pot. When Kelsey found me in the cloakroom, I was getting them to put them back. I was Sir, I promise." Mr Pryce handed her a tissue to wipe away the

The Meeting

tears.

Mr Pryce had no reason to doubt Shan. Her emotions were too strong for her to be lying about this and he always tried to be the person he wished some people had been with him when he got things wrong as a child. Every child deserves to be listened to.

The front door opened and slammed shut. "Helloooo," shouted Mum.

"Right Shan, listen. Thank you for being so honest. I trust you in all you have said and the fact that it has affected you so much since, shows me how much you care. Would you ever do that again?"

"No way, Mr Pryce. I am not a thief. I have never stolen anything before and never will."

"Good. If you really have learned all that you have told me, then your lesson and punishment has already happened. I think we need to be honest and open with your parents too if we want to move on from this. Are you happy with that? Then we can get you back into school where you belong and I am going to set some things up so that you can start making some new friends."

Shan looked scared but nodded just as Mrs Wan entered the room with her cup of coffee and one for Mr Pryce. Mr Wan followed and both parents sat down wondering what this meeting was all about. Mr Pryce began.

As Mr Pryce left, Mrs Wan thanked him very much for his time and care. "Although a part of me is so sorry that Shan did that, I can't tell you how relieved I am that it's finally out in the open and sorted. She must have been so scared dealing with all that on her own. If you ever feel anything else might be worrying Shan in the future, will you please let us know?"

"Of course. Looking back now, I wish I had acted sooner. Thank you for your time Mr and Mrs Wan. Bye Shan."

The Meeting

"Bye," shouted Shan from the living room. Mrs Wan opened the front door.

"What a day!" sighed Mrs Wan. "I feel like the universe is working differently today. Not only with this and with Shan, but on the way home from crawling in lots of traffic, I ended up getting through every green light! That meant I was home much quicker than usual! I hope you have the same luck on your way home too. Thank you again, Mr Pryce. Shan will be back in school tomorrow."

Marlowe Mindful smiled from behind Mum's car keys that were positioned on the table by the front door. Triple mission accomplished. Today had been a good day for all!

Chapter 12
Brain circuits

Shan was amazed at how relieved she felt about everything being out in the open at last. She knew Mum and Dad weren't happy about the stealing, neither was she, but Mr Pryce had been brilliant at explaining things. Shan felt like she had a voice and Mum and Dad seemed to be understanding rather than angry and disappointed, which was what she had expected.

The only thing that today hadn't changed was the fear of going to school tomorrow. It had been over two weeks. She thought back to her last days at school. They couldn't have been worse, but then again she couldn't think of a day that had been enjoyable. Her sad memory bank kicked into action and instantly connected with lots of sad feelings.

Marlowe Mindful noticed the sudden change in Shan and decided that she had one more important job to do today. Shan needed to know about some very important brain functions. She tiptoed over as Shan lay on the settee.

"Hey. That seemed to go pretty well. What are you feeling?" asked Marlowe Mindful.

"Mmm, well I was feeling relieved, happy and positive. I thought Mum and Dad would be really cross. I also thought Mr Pryce was going to shout, but he didn't judge me as being a bad person because I took the erasers. He really listened and that helped so much."

"Your body language and sad face aren't saying upbeat things now though. Is it the thought of school?"

"I sometimes wish I could stay here forever and never have to face all the

Brain Circuits

difficulties of life," said Shan sadly.

"Okay Shan, let's play with that idea, but I think we need to do this in your bedroom so we don't get noticed. Do you agree?"

"Yes, I will tell Mum and Dad I am tidying my room. See you up there."

Marlowe Mindful moved magically to Shan's bedroom and nuzzled down into soft teddy's lap on Shan's bed, ready for them to do some brain work together. Before too long, Shan arrived with a freshly chopped platter of fruit.

"Do you want some?" asked Shan.

"No thanks. I have had an extra treat today already," replied Shan, remembering the traces of toffee sugar syrup on the sweet wrapper in Mr Pryce's bag. You enjoy. So where were we?"

"You had a game in mind," answered Shan, chomping on a crunchy green apple segment.

The Blinks 'Sad'

"Yes, that's right! So let's imagine you really could decide never to go to school again. What would you gain from doing that?"

"Ooh, it would be wonderful," enthused Shan. She then reeled off a very quick list which she wrote down in her favourite pad. It included:

- ✓ I could sleep in every day
- ✓ I wouldn't have to do difficult work
- ✓ I wouldn't have to be around people who don't like me
- ✓ I wouldn't have to face everyone again after what I did
- ✓ I wouldn't get as many things wrong
- ✓ I wouldn't be reminded every day that I am a lonely failure
- ✓ I could eat whenever and whatever I wanted -not packed lunches or school dinners
- ✓ I'd never have to do PE again

"Wow, you did that amazingly quickly, I think you have been thinking about this a lot."

"I have. It is all these thoughts that kept me home, safe here every day."

"Okay. Let's now think about the losses to you and your life if you never went to school again?"

"Mmm, this is hard," pondered Shan. With lots of thought she created a list on the opposite page:

- ✗ I wouldn't learn all about the subjects I do at school
- ✗ I would stop learning about life and people
- ✗ It will be difficult to get a good job if I don't know what I need to know
- ✗ I might get bored being at home every day
- ✗ Mum and Dad might lose their jobs – we then wouldn't have as much

money to do nice things

- ✗ My family, including me, would all be unhappier
- ✗ I would feel an even bigger lonely failure
- ✗ I wouldn't be as healthy
- ✗ I would be more difficult to change

"Interesting," said Marlowe Mindful.

"Very interesting," whispered Shan. "The list of losses is longer isn't it?"

"Yes it is, but look closer. The losses you have listed there have much more serious results for you, your family and your future. Do you see?"

Shan nodded. "Sometimes the easy option isn't always the best, is it? Also if I give up now, all those losses could happen. I need to try harder, but what if I can't do it?"

"You just don't give up until you are where you want to be Shan. Success isn't always based on the end result, it is to do with the hurdles we face and how we overcome them along the way. Imagine what you will feel about yourself tomorrow if you go in to school, knowing how scared you feel now. That is courage and that is success."

Shan nodded a more determined nod this time.

"Yes you are right. I have to do it. I will do it. Mr Pryce will be proud too and he will look out for me. Mum and Dad will be even more proud but I think I will be the proudest!"

"Go you," squealed Marlowe Mindful, dancing as best she could on soft teddy. "There is just one more thing that you need to understand."

Marlowe Mindful went on to explain about everything that Shan needed to do in order to break the low mood of sadness that she had felt for a very long time. She drew a rough sketch of the brain and

The Blinks 'Sad'

showed how many different circuits begin to crash when deep sadness takes over.

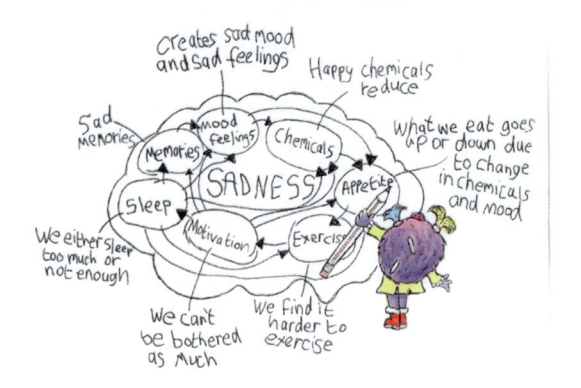

She then drew another picture of the brain which explained how important it was to do certain things differently, even if we don't always feel it, so that the sadness is weakened.

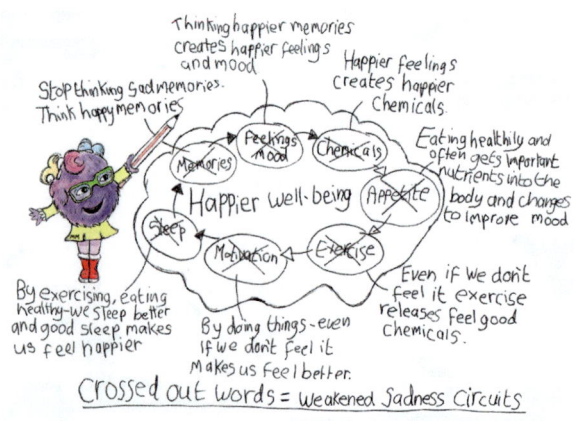

Shan felt like she understood. Sometimes her mum and dad had said that she needed to do things differently, like the other day with breakfast. Today though, she felt like she knew why.

"Thanks Marlowe Mindful, that was brilliant. I feel I have had a tour around my mind and can see what needs to be done now to change this sadness around."

"Just remember that it takes time Shan. In order to change how the brain performs, you need to be the master brain as much as possible and practise all the things that I have taught you as much as possible. Deal?"

"Quadruple deal. Will I see you again?"asked Shan.

"Of course. You have a lot to do over the next few weeks Shan and although I may not see you every day, I will be around watching and checking you are doing okay. I will be here whenever you feel you need me, just shout."

Shan felt full. She felt bursting with understanding and with new things that she could do. She also felt jam-packed with new feelings of positivity and so she hoped more than anything that tomorrow could be the start of a brand new Shan.

Chapter 13
Doing things differently

Shan didn't sleep as well as she hoped that night. Although she had no night terror, her dreams were steered by lots of difficult emotions. One of them jolted her from her sleep.

She had dreamt that she was in school but no-one could see her. When she tried to talk to people they couldn't hear her. When she tried to stand in front of them to get their attention, they looked through her like she didn't exist. Even more weird was that Mr Pryce was wearing a white, sad mask that showed no emotion at all.

This was the scariest part of the dream for Shan as she felt she needed Mr Pryce to be warm and smiley towards her to give her the confidence she needed and to feel like she had someone on her side.

As the dream went on, Shan got smaller and smaller in size. At one point she was stood on top of the pencil pot screaming "Arggggggggghhhhhhhhh" as loud as she could and this is what finally woke her up.

Shan lay there in her darkened room trying to make sense of the dark. As her eyes adjusted, the faint glimmer of the nightlight on the landing began to illuminate familiar objects around her room. She decided to keep her eyes closed in the hope that kinder sleep would come to her next.

What if everyone has forgotten me? thought Shan. What if Mr Pryce was just pretending to be nice? What if everyone really does hate me?

This was the stage where Shan usually stopped when thinking negative thoughts. However, the events of today had taught her do things differently and as Marlowe Mindful said, "If you don't do anything

Doing things differently

differently, nothing will change."

Shan decided to try Stage 2 and answer the *what ifs*!

What if everyone has forgotten me?

- Children's memories are better than that
- It takes a long time to forget someone
- She had only been off for just over two weeks. Polly was once off for 6 months when she went to live in Australia for her dad's job and no-one forgot her

What if Mr Pryce was just pretending to be nice?

- Why would he do that?
- She couldn't remember all of what he said to her earlier but she knew he made her feel better. You can't pretend that
- He has always been her favourite teacher

- He didn't get mean with her when she took the rubbers

What if everyone really does hate me?

- ?
- ?
- ?

This one was a tough one. The problem here was that she hadn't ever showed her classmates the best of her so, truth be known, for them there really wasn't a lot to like. She was determined not to leave this open ended though. She needed to find something that could turn this one around. She tried again.

What if everyone really does hate me?

- Marcus had been kind to her when she was feeling sick with shock the last day she was in school
- Some of the quieter, shy kids in her class had always been nice to her
- Hate was a strong word and she hadn't

been so bad for people to hate her

Although she never felt as confident with this list, she was determined to start tomorrow differently and over time become the person she wanted to be, not the one who was a slave to her sadness.

This thought took Shan back into deep sleep. When she awoke to the sound of her alarm, she felt refreshed. That sleep must have been kinder. The reality of the day ahead, however, was hard and many times Shan felt overwhelmed with emotions that could have slipped her back into bed.

"Don't see today as a big challenge Shan, see it as lots of little steps," chirped Marlowe Mindful from the door handle of the wardrobe.

Shan lifted her head from her hands. "It feels too big to do."

"If you think of it as a whole, it will. So do little bits at a time. Your first hurdle is getting yourself out of bed and into the bathroom. Could you do that?" asked

Marlowe Mindful.

"I don't know."

"Okay, let's look for evidence. Have you ever got out of bed and walked to the bathroom before?"

"Yes."

"So could you get out of bed and walk into the bathroom today?"

"Yes."

"How do you know?" continued Marlowe Mindful.

"Well… I have legs that work, I know the way, and I have done it lots of times before," said Shan lifting herself off her bed.

"Brilliant," said Marlowe Mindful watching Shan head towards the door. "Most times, Shan, the hardest part of doing anything is taking the first step. Hurray for you, you have done it! I believe in you, Shan. I am going to go now but see

Doing things differently

each hurdle as a step closer to where you want to be. See you soon."

When Shan returned from the bathroom, she found putting her uniform on difficult, but she did it. It felt awkward and stiff and very unlike the pyjamas she was so used to wearing these days. She nudged herself forward with every item of clothing. She looked at herself in the mirror. She actually looked quite smart. Her freshly washed uniform made her feel good. Her pride in herself had definitely slipped over the last few months and scrunched up, dirty clothes were often dragged on without care. Today she cared. She entered the kitchen to hear the radio on as normal and Mum and Dad sitting at the table eating cereal.

"Well look at you my darling! You look fabulous! It is so good to see you back with us," beamed Dad.

"I know I always ask you and you say no, but you really should have some breakfast today Shan, to keep your strength up," said Mum, who was also delighted that things felt like they were moving forward at last.

Breakfast wasn't something that she wanted at all. Her tummy was in knots of nervousness but she reminded herself of the importance of fuel to break the sadness cycle.

"Please could I have some banana on toast?" asked Shan. This felt like good food to get her through the trials ahead. It felt like athletes' food and today she needed energy and determination more than ever.

"Of course sweetheart, that is a great idea. Do you want a packed lunch today, or a school dinner?"

Shan hated lunchtimes. This was the time that she usually felt the most sad and lonely. Packed lunches were always better though, as she could sit down and eat it quicker rather than standing alone in the long, boring queue.

"Packed lunch please."

"Banana and toast and a packed lunch coming up."

"How are you feeling today, Shan? asked Dad. I can understand how difficult this could be for you."

Shan smiled a half smile. "I am taking one step at a time Dad, but I feel stronger to do this and also to change some bad habits I have slipped into. I know what I want school to be like now and so I am going to change a few things for the better."

"Well done you! That sounds great!" chorused Mum and Dad together, which made all three of them laugh.

Shan ate her breakfast, packed her bag and made the biggest leap of all by heading out of the front door and on her way to school. She felt very alone and small, just as she had felt in her dream during the night. Everything seemed to be moving very fast. People were passing her and at one point, she wasn't sure if she was moving at all.

"Hi Shan, are you coming in to school today?"

Shan jumped. As she turned to her side, she saw Katie from her class.

"Ermm yes." Shan would have normally ignored her, thinking she was being nosey. Today was a different day so she thought better things.

"Great day to come back on, we have an artist in all afternoon teaching us how to do comic illustrations. I didn't know you lived on this road. I haven't seen you on a morning before. We could walk together from now on if you want. I always walk in on my own too."

"That sounds fun. Yes I have lived here all my life and I would love that. I hate walking to school on my own."

Marlowe Mindful gave an excited wriggle from inside Katie's hood. When she had nipped off earlier, she had gone to do some

Doing things differently

clock tweaking at Katie's house so that she would leave five minutes earlier and then the girls would end up meeting. She then remembered that she needed to head back there and put all the clocks back to the right time before anyone became suspicious.

"I could knock for you tomorrow if you like?" suggested Katie.

Shan nodded enthusiastically. No-one had ever knocked for her, called for her or asked her if she wanted to meet up before. As the girls walked to school, they chatted and chatted about all sorts of things.

Shan told her all about the tummy illness but was also open about the erasers. She explained that she isn't a thief but that she just wasn't thinking properly at that time, and how she was planning to put them back when she was caught by Kelsey.

Katie explained how Mr Pryce had spent a lot of time over the last few weeks talking about the value of learning from mistakes, forgiveness and fresh starts. She then went on to say that he hoped Shan would be back in school soon and how important it was for everyone to be kind to her. This prompted Katie to stop and talk.

Shan's first day back at school couldn't have been better. Mr Pryce welcomed her back warmly. Her classmates showed more kindness to her than they had

Doing things differently

ever done before. Even Kelsey smiled at her and apologised if she had jumped to conclusions. She was also given back her lunchtime job and asked if Katie could do it with her, which was agreed.

As the days and weeks went on, the hurdles got easier and easier and Shan couldn't believe how trouble-free it had all been to turn a sad lonely life around. She regularly reminded herself of the brain circuit's pictures that Marlowe Mindful had drawn for her and how hard she was working to weaken the sadness habits.

Shan began filling her life with happier events, which diluted the time and greatness of her sad thoughts. She also became more trusting with people. She risked being kinder, whereas before she worried that this might be seen as weakness. This developed some nice friendships and even introduced her to some after school clubs.

Shan began to feel trickles of happiness. This could only be a good thing I hear you say, but she made one very big mistake. Shan was beginning to take her happiness for granted and so stopped working so hard on it. Although Marlowe Mindful turned up a few times, Shan was not as interested in what she said, as she thought it was all going well. As the weeks turned into months, old habits began to reappear!

Chapter 14
Back to old ways

Marlowe Mindful was more than aware that this stage would arrive at some point and was actually quite impressed at how Shan had managed for so long to stick to her newly formed behaviours. One day, she decided to make a visit and this one needed to be more demanding.

Over the course of that day, Marlowe Mindful witnessed Shan looking more miserable than normal since making the changes. She had also noticed that her new group of friends (Katie, Etta and Rose, also Noah, Nazim and Johnny from the shy group) were struggling, as Shan didn't want to do as much with them anymore. Breakfast had slipped too and she could see that some brain trails were beginning to disconnect.

Marlowe Mindful found the perfect time to talk to Shan whilst she was walking home from school that night. Katie was being picked up and going to the dentist so Shan was alone, missing her lovely friend, and so engaging in sadder thoughts.

"Hey Shan. How are you doing?" asked Marlowe Mindful.

"Oh, hi Marlowe Mindful. Alright thanks."

"Your face is saying something very different. In fact, I hardly recognise you. Where are you going?"

"What do you mean?" questioned Shan, surprised at what she had just been asked.

"You look the same physically but I can see changes that are taking you back to the old Shan. Is that where you want to go?"

Shan stopped in her tracks. Marlowe

Back to old ways

Mindful was right. She had taken her effort away and was lazily slipping back to a place she really didn't want to go. "Why am I doing this? How do I get back?"

"Come back into the present again. Your past has been pulling you away from everything that is good now. You have stopped noticing it and so you think it isn't there anymore, but it is always there if you value it and want it."

"I don't think my friends like me anymore."

"Is that a guess?" asked Marlowe Mindful.

"Well we don't play as much as we used to. We seem to just sit around."

"That isn't to do with your friends, Shan. They want to play. It is you that has stopped wanting to play. I have heard you say quite a few times, during this week alone, that you can't be bothered. Don't get me wrong, sometimes that is okay if you are genuinely tired or feeling a bit ill. You don't seem like you are either, just that you have lost interest and that activates the sadness again."

"Yes I have said that, but it is how I feel. Then I start worrying that they won't like me for much longer anyway, like everyone else in the past so what's the point."

"Oh dear! We have got ourself into a right pickle, haven't we? You have fallen back into your old pit of doom!

Back to old ways

Shan nodded a weak nod. A car drove past and beeped her. It was shy Nazim, one of her new friends. This reminded her of how far she had come. No-one used to beep her when they passed before. She didn't even know Nazim as he was very shy and probably quite scared of the old Shan. She really didn't want to lose his or the others' friendships.

"Will it always be like this?" asked Shan. "Quite good then awful and then a bit boring and then amazing again?"

"You have just described life, Shan. Yes, it is all of those things at times. However, the harder you work at it and the more you do it, the more natural things begin to feel between the problematic bits."

"Phew! That's good to know at least," said Shan, breathing a sigh of relief at the same time.

"So you have two options. Keep going as you are now with your old habits starting again, or get back on the feel good train

The Blinks 'Sad'

and continue what you were doing before that made you feel happier."

"Where is the train station I need to buy a ticket?" chuckled Shan, very quickly followed by Marlowe Mindful.

"I stopped doing my grateful list as well," said Shan.

"I know you did, but it is easy to start again. I tried to tell you before but at the time, you didn't think you needed it. Sometimes the hardest part of my job is having to let time take its course. You will always do something better if you want to, from the inside rather than someone else telling you."

"But I have done it, haven't I? I have now learned the lesson again but from the inside. Does this mean I will do it better next time?"

"Not necessarily, but if you keep mindful about it and grateful at the same time, then you are more likely to keep doing it because it is *about you* and *for you*."

Back to old ways

Shan went on to tell Marlowe Mindful all the things that she was going to do again tomorrow, starting the day with breakfast followed by playing again, even if she didn't always feel like it. She was also going to work harder at not listening to old Shan when she popped up.

Marlowe Mindful was happy again. She also suggested that now might be a good time to bring Mum and Dad on board and for Shan to stick to her part in rule number one of the Blinks' stages.

Shan agreed. Mum and Dad had been so supportive of her over the last few months and also seemed much happier in themselves too. She didn't want them to slip back either. So that night over tea, she told them of the journey she had been on for the last few months and how the last few weeks had started to become quite bumpy again.

Mum and Dad were so proud of Shan and noted how mature she had become throughout this difficult time. They all looked back for a moment to when Shan stayed in bed for that two weeks! The difference was amazing. Like her parents, Shan wanted it to stay that way. Mum and Dad promised her that they would always support her, however she was feeling. Shan promised to be as open as she could with them so that they could always be the best help to her.

Marlowe Mindful left on a wave of contentment. She could feel Stage 5 approaching, though another few weeks' observation would be the ultimate decider.

Nevertheless, Marlowe Mindful felt a positivity in her gut reaction system that made her feel confident in Shan's outcome. Shan was no longer alone in her sadness and was also skilled up from the inside in order to drive her sadness out of town and learn to live on happy street.

Shan also felt proud and strong again, but this time in a different way. It felt like those feelings were deeper inside her and more entwined into who she felt she now was. Pride and strength were beginning to feel familiar and she hoped that one day, they would feel normal. At one time, she would have said 'only time will tell' but like you, me, and a team of small fluffy folk, Shan now knows it takes a lot more than that, doesn't it?

Chapter 15
New friends, new lifestyles

As time passed, the changes in Shan got better and better. She learned to accept her sadness, which was huge in her learning to do things differently and achieve emotional freedom. As the sadness slowly disappeared, she felt like she made room for happier feelings, which became a magnet to new friendships and strengthened existing ones.

Shan's journey didn't go without problems and this is important for all of us to know. This isn't a fairy tale where everything is always wonderful and people live happily ever after! This is a reality tale.

Life has many moments of wonderfulness, excitement and amazingness, which we must hold on to and lock away inside us. At times, life can also be peppered with ordinary, sometimes boring and unpleasant times too. It is during these difficult times that we are tested the most. It is the most difficult times in our lives that help us to understand how lucky we are when life is good.

Katie was accelerated to Shan's number one best friend. Living so close to each other had really helped their friendship grow. Not only did they continue to walk to and from school together, they regularly popped to each other's houses on a weekend and the list of things they had in common grew alongside Shan's self-confidence.

They began a trampoline class together on Tuesdays after school and their parents took turns to take them and pick them up. Sometimes it would involve tea at each other's houses too. Shan found that she had many things in common with Katie that only time could highlight, including music, films and showbiz gossip!

They also started writing a play together. This did cause some arguments, especially when their directing vision began to differ. In the early days, Shan used to stomp off in frustration. The stomping didn't really help but after several minutes of deep in, hold, and out breathing, she was able to return and continue like a true professional. Both girls found a way to compromise and meet in the middle.

After a while, Shan didn't even need to stomp. She was able to breathe through her annoyances without anyone seeming to notice. They managed to rehearse the play with their friends as the cast and even show it to the infants at Christmas, which received enthusiastic applause.

The best thing about their friendship, however, was that they shared problems and secrets with each other. Shan told Katie things that she had never told anyone before, not even her mum and dad. Katie also found Shan to be amazingly wise and always seemed to know how to make problems better. I wonder who she learned that skill from?!

Sometimes, Shan felt disloyal for not sharing the Blinks' magic with Katie. On several occasions, she felt like she was going to burst if she didn't tell her best friend about Marlowe Mindful. This was one of Shan's toughest challenges but she never regretted not doing it, as she knew that by keeping the secret, help was always available for Katie too.

Shan also got into playing football and was selected for the school team. She found this accelerated her to a new status of respect with some of the boys in her class, although not quite everyone felt that way. Some of her classmates tried to make fun of Shan saying that she must really be a boy! As you can imagine, this upset Shan.

What it didn't do, was upset her enough to make her think about not doing it. She could see that the unkind kids were

New friends, new lifestyles

trying to rob her of her enjoyment and happiness, but she wasn't going to allow this. This came only after some help from Marlowe Mindful, who reminded Shan that people and situations can only trigger emotions, we decide how much emotional energy we give to situations.

By recognising this early on, Shan didn't become deeply unhappy about being teased, as maybe once she would have done. She didn't let herself spend hours overthinking it or guessing what she thought the boys were thinking about her. Due to this, Shan's mood didn't drop too low and so her motivation to play football didn't change either. She also had the last laugh when she was scouted at a school football game and taken on by Sheffoold United Football Club to be part of their girls' team. Shan also had a story written about her in the local newspaper!

Shan never ever forgot Mr Pryce's role in how things had moved on either. She thought many times about all the reasons he was her favourite teacher. Sometimes she struggled to remember the things he said to her that moved the situation on, but she never forgot, and would ever forget, how much better he made her feel.

Mr Pryce showed he cared when she was struggling to feel anything positive. He had activated Shan's responsibility with the store cupboard job and that was one of the best feelings she had ever felt. She continued to build on this by taking on other jobs around school and always doing them as best she could.

Things at home also improved for Shan. She felt like she had a closer connection with her parents. When Shan's sadness had dominated her feelings, it sometimes felt like she was locked inside herself and could not reach out to anyone. This had added to the loneliness.

The Wan family now made sure that most times of the week, they sat down to eat breakfast and evening meal together. Shan would never know how much her breakfast had an impact on her mood, but it definitely did. By fuelling up before school, her body was able to work as best as possible and had the energy it needed to be the greater Shan.

This time together also kept conversations flowing and was a time for Mum and Dad to notice if Shan's mood was changing. They shared teatime tales of things from across the day and made emotions a part of that. They also did more things together and Shan found that seeing her parents happier made her feel better, and vice versa.

The only time that Shan was reminded of the old 'her' was when she was tired. This brought back lots of negative feelings that she really didn't like anymore. On those days she felt grumpy, flat and generally less 'Shan'.

Shan had started going to bed later and only just coming off her tablet screen before climbing the stairs. She was also getting lazy at cleaning her teeth and just flopping into bed, hoping that sleep would magically arrive.

On several nights, Shan laid there scanning her messy room in the semi-darkness. She had swapped her pillows recently and so wasn't half as comfortable as she used to be. This led to lots of wriggling and moving around until she finally found the best position.

One night Marlowe Mindful decided to make one last visit to try and conquer this remaining trouble spot. "Hey you, wriggler. How are you?"

"Hi Marlowe Mindful, lovely to see you, it has been ages. Things are going really well thanks. My life is so different, but I am sure you know that?"

"Yes I do and it is great, you have worked so hard. Well done. I thought it might be worth me popping and seeing you one last time as so many areas are going well, but sleep still seems to be the last thing we need to sort."

New friends, new lifestyles

"Oh yes, please. That would be so very helpful. I don't know what's gone wrong but my sleep seems to be worse now than ever."

"You have got into some bad pre-sleep habits and until we change some of them, your sleep won't improve."

"Really, like what?" asked a confused Shan.

"You humans seem to take sleep for granted. Sleep is something that we need to prepare for in order to make it as good quality as possible."

"Oh, I just thought that you got into bed and then you eventually go to sleep."

"So do many, Shan. Here are some things you need to do." Marlowe Mindful pulled out from her pocket a small piece of paper that magically became A4 size when she rubbed the paper between her small hands. The sheet of paper fell into Shan's lap. On it was a list of pre-sleep routines written in Marlowe Mindful's handwriting.

It included:

> *Top tips for improved sleep!*
>
> ✔ *Come off screens at least an hour before bed so that your brain is less stimulated with blue light*
> ✔ *Turn the big light off in the living room and your bedroom too so that your brain registers it is night time*
> ✔ *Always have a bedtime routine to move you from your daytime to sleep time - never forget to brush your teeth!*
> ✔ *It is difficult to sleep if your bedroom is too hot, cold or messy (your brain likes things to be right to go to sleep)*
> ✔ *Write down any worries and leave them on the paper till the morning. Your brain can't sleep if it is thinking, planning or sorting!*
> ✔ *Get comfy. Your mind feels stressed if you are uncomfortable*
> ✔ *Relax! You can't sleep well if you keep moving about. Find a comfy position and breathe into wonderful sleep*

New friends, new lifestyles

"Oh my goodness," said Shan. "I don't do any of that."

"I know, but you are not alone. If you try all of these things then, over time, your sleep will get a lot better and so will your mood."

"Thanks Marlowe Mindful, you know I will," replied Shan. "This feels like more than a goodbye tonight."

"I think it is," said Marlowe Mindful, trying hard to hide her welling up eyes.

"I really couldn't have done any of this without you, Marlowe Mindful, I really couldn't," said Shan, also brushing away the tears.

"You did all the hard work Shan, not me. You could have done nothing, and nothing would have changed. All the credit goes to you and I genuinely mean that."

"I'm not sure I agree, but it is good to know that I am in charge of what I think and feel, and who I want to be."

"Absolutely Shan. The future doesn't just happen. You create it. I am very proud of you. Keep up the good work!"

Shan wrapped her fingers round Marlowe Mindful and gently pulled her up towards her dampened cheek to show her love and appreciation.

"I will never forget this time we have had together and I will never forget you. By working hard on the things you have

New friends, new lifestyles

taught me, I can keep you alive in my heart every day."

"Thank you Shan. I feel happy to go and start finding my next child. You have passed the final test. You now believe in yourself and your abilities. Goodbye Shan and thank you for letting me share your journey with you."

And with that, Marlowe Mindful was gone.

Shan didn't know what the tears were about. Were they happiness that she had reached where she needed to be? Or sadness that she would no longer see her little friend? Relief that she had got to where she wanted to be, or pride that she had achieved what once seemed like an impossible goal?

Whatever her tears meant, they made Shan feel very alive in that moment and she felt awesome. She decided to have that as her last waking thought. She fluffed up her pillow, nestled down under her duvet and let the night time take her to the happy place she had discovered.

Chapter 16
The future

Marlowe Mindful loved it when a project was completed, though she always found them very difficult to end. Working with Shan had taught her a lot. Once again, she had learned how tough it was to be a kid sometimes. Shan had been a pleasure to work with and although she was missing her, knew that it was for all the right reasons. Missing Shan meant that she had passed with flying colours and made the progress she needed to be a happier person.

As she was lying around relaxing with her other Blink friends, who had also completed their projects, an interesting conversation sprung up. It was to do with Blink magic.

The Blinks 'Sad'

"Do you think we really are magic?" asked Claudia Charming.

A gasp rang out from the other Blinks. "Of course we are. Never doubt Blink magic!"

"Don't get me wrong, I know we use our skills well and we get good results, but is it all us?" continued Claudia Charming.

"I was just thinking exactly the same, Claudia Charming," began Marlowe Mindful. "I have just been working with a wonderful girl called Shan and she has worked so hard at changing how she feels. I only made the suggestions, she did all the hard work. I think she had a special magic too. A magic that made her not give up, even at the most difficult times."

The rest of the Blinks started nodding in agreement and reflecting on the young people they too had just been working with.

"Yes, my child had the same ability to work on his issues. He showed real courage," said Halleemah Happier-Times.

"Mine too," added Bradley Brave.

"Maybe the magic occurs when the right combination of Blink and child meet?" suggested Mila Motivated.

An energy of nodding exploded amongst the Blinks, who then collapsed into sighs of contentment. Marlowe Mindful loved being a Blink but she knew she wouldn't have a job if it wasn't for the ace kids out there who were open to little nudges towards better times.

Shan never looked back. Well actually she did, but only now and then to remind her of how far she had come. Sometimes she slipped into her faulty setting but because it felt so unusual now to what she felt most days, she noticed it quickly and did her best to skip away from her old ways.

Shan had become the person she wanted to be. A person who she liked and who was creating a life of achievements, successes, lovely people and happier memories. She never quite forgot all her sad memories but she did learn to recognise that the past was the past and there was very little she could do about that. So that was where the sad thoughts needed to stay.

For the first time ever, the future looked exciting. However, she never, ever took the good things of the day for granted. Marlowe Mindful had taught Shan the importance of being in the moment and appreciating the things that we feel lucky for as often as possible. Every night before Shan went to sleep, she reminded herself of things that had occurred over the day that had put a smile on her face. Most days, Shan could name at least five nice things. Her record was nine!

Some days, Shan struggled to think of three good things but on those days, she looked back in her happiness book and found day after day of lovely things that had made her feel nice. That always made her feel better in that moment and sent her to sleep feeling positive, which usually triggered a better day afterwards.

Shan also continued with making sure that she did as much as possible to prevent the dark mood getting too close again. She continued eating a healthy diet, and always had something to eat when she came in from school, to boost her energy and her mood. She stayed active and took part in exercise every week to keep her brain circuits working well.

The top tips for sleep also became something that she knew off by heart.

Over time, the piece of paper Marlowe Mindful had given her became very wrinkly and scruffy. It even had a spell with her mum when she too was struggling to sleep. When Shan's mum asked her where it had come from, she simply replied "A very special friend."

The main difference in Shan was the improved relationships she felt. Shan could happily say that she had some very good friends. Katie stayed a very close and special friend to Shan. In fact, they called each other 'best ever friends'. This also kept the sadness at bay as the lonelier you are, the more time you have to think about how sad and lonely you are! With the support of her family, these friendships also helped her carry out rule number 1 when working with the Blinks. Shan didn't store up difficult feelings anymore. She realised she felt better much more quickly if she got them out to weaken how difficult they feel.

Shan had started giving herself to the

The future

right sort of people and they seemed to like it, which meant she gave more in return and so it went on. Shan also loved being nice, regardless of what others thought of her.

Sometimes the haters tried to remind her of the past, as if she was now a fake. At those times, she remembered Marlowe Mindful more than ever. She recalled Marlowe Mindful once telling her that even if you don't feel like it, if you smile, your brain thinks something good must be happening so releases happy chemicals.

So at times like that, Shan would smile and breathe in deeply, thanking the universe that she was no longer like them and no longer like that. What was doubly amazing was that doing that always helped, as if it was a special formula to protect her inner feelings.

At those times, somewhere there in that enormous universe, a small, good hearted, funky ball with green glasses would feel something whizz through her purple fluff.

The Blinks 'Sad'

Whatever it was, no-one really knows, but it definitely had a positive vibe to it and was a reminder that we are all capable of making our lives what we want them to be, because the future doesn't just happen, *you* create it!

The End for now...

Acknowledgements

As with all the Blinks' books, there are many people behind the scenes who are a huge part in getting these books ready for production. To my fabulous Auntie Karin, who was the first person on the planet to ever read a finished book; her proofreading and critique I value more than she will ever know. To Lily, my amazing daughter who does all the amends and a final proofread, to Jill who reins me in when my psychologist brain takes over, and to Janet my amazing proof reader who keeps me on point with punctuation and grammar. Ladies you are an invaluable team, thank you so very much.

Thank you also to Rachel Pesterfield for her creative mind and skilled illustrations which pepper the book with colour to feed the imagination of the reader. A special thanks also to Gail who is constantly thinking of new ways to get the Blinks' books out there.

Thank you again to Hallam FM's Cash 4 Kids, for sponsoring 'The Blinks' and aiming to get copies into every primary school in South Yorkshire.

I would also like to say a huge thank you to my beautiful mum who has taught me all I know. Thank you Mum, I wouldn't be doing any of this without your foundations of love, support and belief. My forever thanks also to my sister, who really is the best sister in the whole world.

I would also like to thank Wendy B who, after purchasing book 1 – Worry, for her granddaughter Amelie Soffia, has become a true Blinks' fan. I truly appreciate your kindness and advocacy of this series.

I would also like to recognise the wonderful people who have moved on from our lives this year. Some are people I know personally, some are special to those I care about and some are creative legends. Please share a moment to remember David, Mick, Pam, Carrie Fisher and George Michael.

About The Author
Andrea Chatten - MSc, MBPsS,
PGCL&M, BEd(Hons), Dip.CBT

Andrea Chatten has been a specialised teacher for over 25 years, working with children from ages 5-16 with emotional and behavioural difficulties. She is currently working as 'Lead Children's Emotional & Behavioural Psychologist' at Unravel CEBPC with schools and families in Sheffield.

Developing positive, trusting relationships has always been at the heart of her practice with children and young people in order to nudge them into improved psychological well-being. Over the years, Andrea has developed and applied many positive developmental psychology approaches.

This insight is incorporated into her stories in order to help children, young people and their families to gain more of an understanding and potential strategies to try, in order to deal with a range of behavioural issues that children and young people could experience.

Andrea created 'The Blinks' so that parents could also benefit from reading the books with their children, particularly if they identify with the children in the stories and their family circumstances. Both parent and child can learn how to manage early forms of psychological distress as a natural part of growing up rather than it become problematic when not addressed in its early stages.

The Blinks' is a series of books that discreetly apply lots of psychological theory throughout the story including

Cognitive Behavioural Therapy, Developmental and Positive Psychology approaches.

This first book in the series tackles the issue of worry and how to prevent this everyday cognition from becoming more serious anxiety in the future.

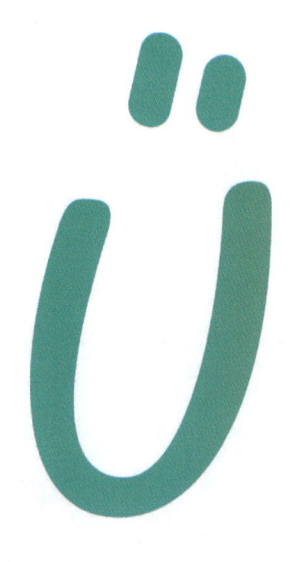

www.unravelcebpc.co.uk

Facebook - /Theblinksbooks

Twitter - @BlinksThe

THE BLINKS REFERENCE MANUALS

Accompanying each of 'The Blinks' novels is a Reference Manual for parents, carers, older siblings, teachers, and professionals.

The supporting manual for each novel provides a greater understanding of the psychology of each title; worry, anger, self-esteem, and sadness (other titles are being created) and how it can impact on emotional developmental and well-being.

It also provides lots of 'top tips' on what works best for children and young people whilst growing up and some activity questions that can be used as a starting point to initiate emotive dialogue or discussion.

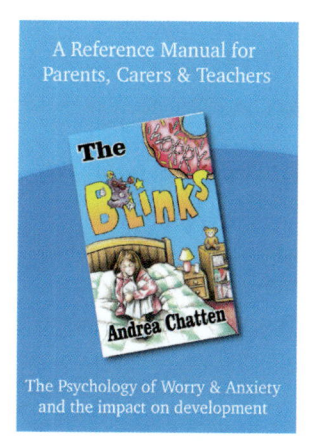

The Blinks
"Worry"
Reference Manual

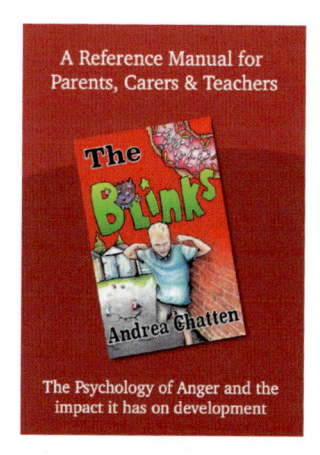

The Blinks
"Anger"
Reference Manual

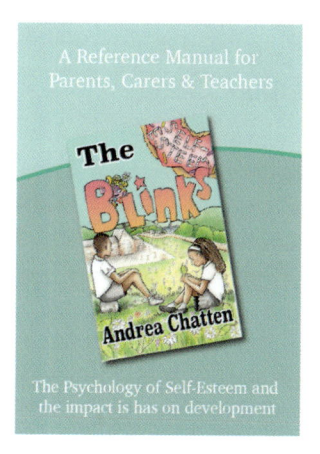

The Blinks
"Self-Esteem"
Reference Manual

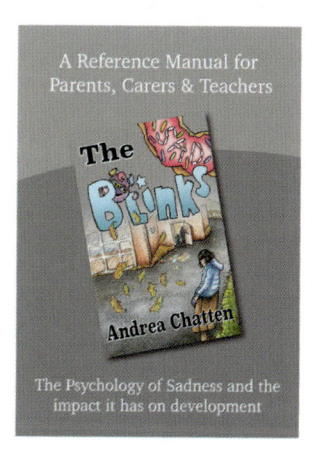

The Blinks
"Sad"
Reference Manual

OTHER TITLES IN THE BLINKS SERIES OF NOVELS

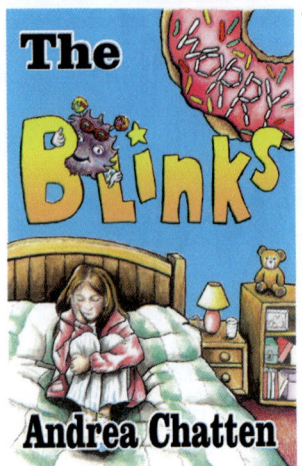

The Blinks - Worry

When Amanda is discussed at the midnight meeting, she is lucky to become part of some very special Blink intervention. As a result, Amanda begins to make changes she never thought possible.

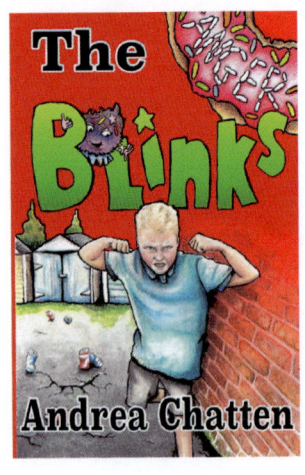

The Blinks - Anger

Robbie's life has never been great, but the events over the last few years have slowly made him more and more unhappy and angry. One day it all gets too much, and his anger erupts! Through a series of events, Robbie learns just who is responsible for his anger and how to deal with it.

The Blinks - Self-Esteem

Bladen and Tim are twins who have spent many years being unkind to each other. This has not helped them to develop very positive feelings. Their low self-esteem has affected their confidence, friendships, and their happiness. Larry Love-Who-You-Are recognises works hard to help the twins overcome some very personal challenges.

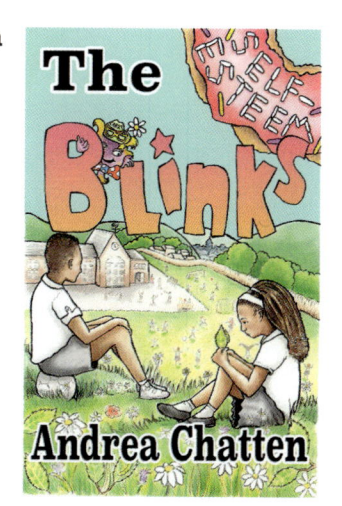

The Blinks - Sad

Shan is a normal girl who has a normal life in many way, but one thing Shan has which many other children don't have is buckets and buckets of sadness. Thankfully, Marlowe Mindful sees Shan as someone who is ready for Blinks' support and begins the process of helping her understand her sadness and how to change her feelings for the better.

COMING SOON – The Blinks – 'Shy'.

IN ORDER TO PURCHASE ANY OF THE BLINKS NOVELS OR MANUALS PLEASE GO TO:
www.theblinks.co.uk